D0893611

EARL CAMPBELL

EARL CAMPBELL

Houston Oiler Superstar

Betty Lou Phillips

David McKay Company, Inc.

New York

For
Brian, Keene, Bryce, Bruce,
Toby, Robbie, and John

With special thanks and warm appreciation to Earl Campbell and his mother,
Ann; the Houston Oilers; John Phillips and Bruce; Dr. Earl C. Kinzie;
Alleen Willis; Georgia Greaney and Maurice Greening; Jerry Reid,
Sam Pierson, Jr.; Joyce Ferguson, Ann Straus; and last, but far from
least, Glenn Bradley, Alex Whitney, Joe Fortin, Bob Palmer, Sharon
Kitter, Chuck Bloodgood, Linda Green, and Amy Berkower.

Library of Congress Cataloging in Publication Data

Phillips, Betty Lou.
  Earl Campbell, Houston Oiler superstar.

  Includes index.
  SUMMARY: A biography of the Heisman Trophy winner
who became Rookie of the Year and Player of the Year
in professional football.
  1. Campbell, Earl—Juvenile literature.
2. Football players—United States—Biography—
Juvenile literature. [1. Campbell, Earl. 2. Football
players. 3. Afro-Americans—Biography] I. Title.
GV939.C36P47   796.33'2'0924 [B] [92] 79-2269

ISBN 0-679-20603-5

  3 4 5 6 7 8 9 10

Manufactured in the United States of America

CONTENTS

They challenged him on the day of the 1978 draft—when the Houston Oilers made him the nation's No. 1 pick—with questions like "How do you think you'll measure up against running back standouts Tony Dorsett, O. J. Simpson, and Jimmy Brown?"

Right away, Earl Campbell set them straight: "I don't think it's a good idea to look at somebody and say, 'I'd like to be just like him.' I've never wanted to do that. You need to be yourself, not copy somebody. I've always tried to be just Earl Campbell."

Earl Campbell, with a story all his own.

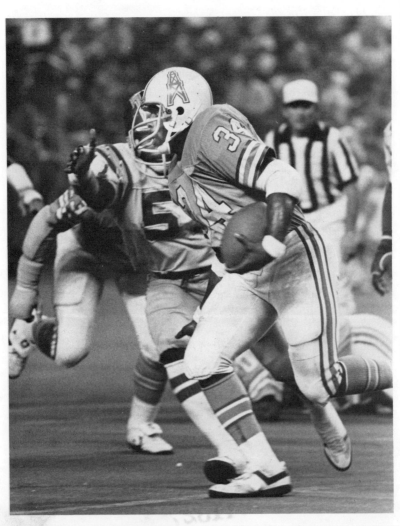

1 / *Mama's Roses*

Earl Christian Campbell was born March 29, 1955, in Tyler, Texas, a town 220 miles northwest of Houston, the biggest city in the state. The family doctor, Earl Christian Kinzie, weighed Earl in at eight pounds, two ounces. Then Dr. Kinzie gave him the first of many physicals—all of them free because Earl was named after the doctor.

"Little Earl" was the sixth of Ann and B. C. Campbell's eleven children. Together with four sisters and six brothers, he grew up sleeping three in a bed in an unpainted house at the end of a winding country road, five miles north of Tyler.

The little house in the Swan community was not meant to accommodate thirteen people. In truth, it looked worn and aging in 1965 when the Campbells moved in. The roof leaked, plaster was falling from the ceiling, and paper was peeling from the walls. The five rooms were warmed only by a small gas space heater in the corner of one room.

When the weather turned cold, Earl's father took clothing from the closets and covered his freezing children, who huddled together. On nights when the sky was filled with stars, they could look up from their beds and see the

Doctor Earl Christian Kinzie delivered Earl at home. (Gregg Burger)

The Campbell home in Tyler, Texas. (Gregg Burger)

Big Dipper. Nothing could be done about that, for there was no money to repair the holes in the tin roof on the house. Still, Earl's father had good intentions of repairing the house as best he could. In fact, he promised he would—when he wasn't driving a truck, taking on odd jobs, and growing roses to support his large family. And no doubt he would have—as soon as he finished installing a bathroom in the house to replace the privy out back. B. C. Campbell's word meant something. But he never had time to keep his word. When Earl was in the fourth grade, his father died of a heart attack, leaving his wife with all the responsibilities the two had once shared.

While the rest of his family were open in their grief, Earl was sad and silent. He'd miss following his daddy around, but he strained to hide his feelings. Rather sadly, Earl's mother didn't have time to mourn. She had roses to grow, white people's houses to clean, and eleven children to raise by herself.

Ann Collins Campbell grew up in Smith County, less than a five-minute drive from where she now lived. As a girl, she was bused into Tyler to the all-black Emmett Scott High School. A month after graduation in 1942, she married and started a family. Now, there would be no looking back.

After her husband's funeral, Ann Campbell took a deep breath and gathered her children around her on their unsteady porch. Softly and slowly, she talked to them, her kind face grim with worry. She reminded them that she was by herself now and needed their help. What the future would bring was unclear. Yet, somehow she would clothe and feed them and send them to school.

"But if you get into trouble," she said firmly, "I can't

afford to pay no fines. I'll put my best foot forward and expect the same from you children." Next, she told the children what they'd have to do to make it through the coming dark times. "We'll all go to church and Sunday school each week," she said, "and we'll work hard and stay busy."

The only thing that troubled Earl was losing his father. He was accustomed to waking up early on Sunday morning and going to church. All the Campbell children had a sound, church-going background because their parents were deeply religious Baptists who didn't believe in fighting or swearing. Although he was only nine, Earl was accustomed to working hard and staying busy. From the time he was four years old, he spent most hot, muggy days in the rose fields. While other children his age were taking their naps, Earl was hauling water and budding the tender new rose bushes. He was also growing strong from tilling the two acres of roses that his parents tended and sold.

As it happened, the Campbells lived in the Rose Capital of America. Tyler's rose fields, large and small, turn out over 500 varieties of the flower and produce more than half of the country's supply. Each year, nearly 750,000 people from every state in the Union, as well as many foreign countries, visit Tyler to witness the flowers' beauty. Earl, however, didn't enjoy the rose fields. Whenever there was talk about roses, they were "mama's roses," as far as he was concerned. And that's what he called them, as he struggled to rearrange the soil. But there was no bitterness on Earl's part. He understood why he was there.

"Working in the rose fields was just like going to school," recalls Earl. "I didn't like going to school, but I knew I had to do it."

4

Raising roses was a serious business for the Campbells. They depended upon the flowers for their livelihood. Even if they hadn't, Mrs. Campbell felt it was her obligation to teach each of her children how to work. This would be an important factor in their lives.

Despite his understanding, Earl has confessed, "I'd always do something to try to get out of working in the fields. I'd rather have been picking watermelons. Then, if I had a watery taste in my mouth, all I'd have to do is bust one."

Earl worked in the middle of a shadeless field because that's what the rest of his family did. "It was like we were all a team," he says. "My family was always my team."

When there was work to be done—hauling hay, picking peas, berries, or roses—all the family pitched in to do their share. But when the sun shone blindingly over Tyler, there was no doubt that Earl would have preferred to be elsewhere. Like most folks in Texas, he was partial to hunting and fishing.

"We'd go out in the rose fields and work, and Earl would always want to quit," his mother clearly recalls. "He'd be *so* tired. Until he'd come home."

Then Earl was never too tired to play football.

"He'd be out in the yard, throwing the football around, full of energy," said Ann Campbell.

2 / *Mama Changes Her Mind*

From the first moment he was introduced to a football, Earl was interested in learning about the game. But Ann Campbell did her best to "disencourage" her sons from playing football when they were growing up. The fact is, she tried to steer them away from all sports—partly because of her protective nature, but mostly because if they were hurt, there wouldn't be any dimes to spare for doctors' bills. The family was already living on a tight budget. Moreover, the prospects for Ann Campbell's earning more money as a maid were not good.

Rather than risk upsetting their mama, Earl and his brothers played football down the road whenever they could slip away. At first, Mrs. Campbell was unaware that they were playing ball with the town's "winos." But she was very concerned with the upbringing of her children, and she soon discovered what was going on. In spite of her disapproval, she gave in to her sons' desires—at least somewhat.

Tending the rose farm almost the year 'round, doing the necessary chores, and attending church and school left very little time for sports. Yet, when Mrs. Campbell realized she couldn't discourage her sons' interest in athletics, she decided she "had to join them." Accordingly, she called a family conference to work out the problem before it became a crisis.

"You can choose *one* sport," Mrs. Campbell said one sweltering evening when the hush that precedes a storm was settling in.

Earl nodded happily as he raised his eyes to look up at his mama. For him, choosing one sport wasn't an easy decision to make, however. He loved to run, and so he thought about going out for track. He liked to play basketball, too. But most of all, he wanted to play football, Earl realized. Ever since he had first played flag football, when he was in the fourth grade at Griffin Elementary, he had thought about playing as well as Dick Butkus, the Chicago Bears' ferocious middle linebacker. Becoming a professional football player was already on Earl's mind, but he didn't talk about this with anyone. Most of the time, he kept his feelings to himself.

As it was, Earl's life as a football player got off to a running start: running five miles was the way he got home from practice after the school bus left the grounds at the end of the day. Frequently, stray dogs tried to stop him. Earl was fast, though, and when necessary, he defended himself with a belt wrapped around his wrist. There were times when his body ached and his feet bled as he raced down country road 492 in his wet clothes. Yet Earl never complained. He was doing what he wanted most. Except for his family, there was nothing Earl loved more than football.

At Moore Junior High School, coach Laurence La-Croix inspired his seventh, eighth, and ninth-grade players with enthusiasm for the game. And Earl stood out from the group. His determination to succeed and his willingness to work were apparent.

As the coach taught him how to handle the football, he was impressed by Earl's eagerness. "You're going to play only as well as you practice," LaCroix said. "If you make a lot of mistakes in practice, you're going to do the same in a game."

Heeding this advice, Earl worked tirelessly to become an outstanding linebacker. Before long, in game after game, he was bursting into opposing backfields, making punishing tackles, and building a reputation for toughness and speed.

By the time Earl was a freshman, Coach LaCroix was certain that the boy's future lay in football. One day, La-Croix asked Billy Newsome, the Baltimore Colt all-pro defensive lineman, to come in and talk with the coach's teams. LaCroix had coached Newsome at Jacksonville before moving west to Tyler.

That day, it was Earl's turn to be impressed. "I could see in his eyes that he was and that he wanted to be like Billy," recalls LaCroix.

Nevertheless, Earl missed practice on occasion, and he talked back to his coach. Although he was quiet (except when he was around boys his own age), he generally spoke his mind to LaCroix. Earl felt close to him; LaCroix had become a father figure as well as one of Earl's best friends. In truth, Earl could not have chosen a better friend and model.

"Sure," says Coach LaCroix, "Earl would miss practice like other young players do, and he'd talk back, too. But he was extremely coachable."

Earl responded well to instruction. Under the coach's watchful eye, he began to show the depth of his desire and drive—a mighty drive that would one day stun the sports world and lead him to national celebrity.

3 / *Bad Earl*

Just as it appeared that Earl might be developing into a great athlete, just when it seemed he was taking his first steps toward becoming a professional football player, Earl ran into some problems. Indeed, it seemed as if his opportunities might disappear along with his hopes.

For a while, Ann Campbell was certain that "Earl was going over fool's hill. He started smoking cigarettes and drinking a little beer. He got kind of wild," says his mother, though he never experimented with drugs.

During his early teens, he was also shooting craps and hustling pool. Sometimes he went looking for games; sometimes he didn't. Either way, he sometimes made as much as $100 at the tavern down the road. Being a "pool shark" won him the respect of admiring friends, who called him "Bad Earl." And Earl referred to himself by the same name.

"I was on the path to the penitentiary," he notes cheerlessly.

His mother had other hopes, however. She saw potential in Earl, and she was ready to back up her conviction in order to prevent her son's talent from going to waste. Although she had given in to his longing to compete in athlet-

9

ics, she stubbornly refused to permit him to continue running around with a group she didn't like. When she sat Earl down, Ann Campbell did some fast and serious talking. "Get 'hold of yourself," she said firmly. "If you do, you can go places in life.

"It's awful tough to pick up where a dad should be doing the talking," Mrs. Campbell volunteers. But at the time, she didn't have a choice. She wanted her message to be loud and clear. And it was. Today Earl remembers: "My mom told me that I was something special, that God had given me a talent. She said I could go on and use that blessing, get an education, and play professional football. But I couldn't do any of those things if I kept on doing what my friends were doing."

4 / *Finding Himself*

Whether friends are good, bad, or indifferent, walking out on them is far from easy. To be sure, finding oneself is even harder. Yet Earl knew that if he didn't change his ways, it would be to his everlasting detriment, for he could never blame the fact that he was poor on a lack of opportunity to better himself.

One evening, when the cries of crickets were echoing through the hills, Earl leaned against a tall, stately pine tree near his home and prayed. "I said, 'Lord, I can't help myself. Would you take over?' " he remembers. "And it all just started happening."

What happened was that Earl was blessed with size, power, balance, and speed. And that was just the beginning. In his first varsity game for John Tyler High School, eight times he sacked Longview's quarterback, Jeb Blount, behind the line of scrimmage. Eight times—all unassisted— and he was credited with pressuring the passer even more. A week later, he drove hard and tackled the Marshall ball carrier behind the goal line for a two-point safety. The season was nowhere near over, but away Earl went, rolling down and plowing over the opposition. Earl Campbell was on his way.

Oddly enough, when he arrived at Rose Stadium for his first game, October 9, 1971, he found that his name wasn't on the roster. By the end of the year, however, his name was well known. Earl drew even more attention during his sophomore and junior years when he was named the district's defensive player of the year as a linebacker.

In Earl's senior year at John Tyler High, Coach Corky Nelson and assistant coach LaCroix made an important change. Over Earl's objections, they moved him to halfback because that's where he was needed.

Earl was comfortable as a linebacker—the position he wanted to play. But he stopped complaining after he spoke his mind. For his new position, Earl trained harder than ever on his own—running, lifting weights, conditioning himself. He also kept his part of the bargain by working in the rose fields every night; then he polished his skills by throwing the ball around with his brothers.

All the hard work paid off. What's more, Earl learned to like his new position. The coaches were counting on that and a lot more. And the 5-feet 11-inch, 214-pound strong man didn't let them down. When he started running, it looked as if he'd never stop. During his senior year, he rushed for a breathtaking 2,037 yards—running 40 yards in 4.6 seconds and outracing would-be tacklers. Swift and sure, Earl led his school to victory after victory through a 15–0 season. In his last year at John Tyler, the team won every game they played, including the 1973 Class AAAA Championship over Austin's Reagen High in Houston's spacious Astrodome.

One time, Earl ran for a touchdown in practice and did a funky dance in the end zone, swaying his knees in and out. His old friend coach LaCroix took Earl aside and

12

Earl finished his high school career in the Astrodome and dreamed of returning to Houston's "Eighth Wonder of the World." (Sam Pierson, Jr.)

told him that he didn't have to show off to attract attention to his ability. "People are going to see and read about you anyway," LaCroix said, as Earl took the criticism to heart, not even sure why he had acted like a hotshot.

At the next game, Earl was eager to score. When he did, he simply handed the ball to the referee with no knee-wobbling or ball-spiking.

That night, Conroe High School head coach, W. T. Stapler, had put up an eleven-man line. In one seven-yard run Earl made against the Tigers, it took ten different hits to bring him down.

"I'm not saying all ten tacklers hit him. But they had shots at him," said the Conroe coach. "He ran past two tacklers at the line of scrimmage. Then he spun and spun around till somebody else got a shot at him. I know it sounds impossible, but we've got film to prove it. I always thought Superman wore a cape and a red and blue suit. I was wrong. He wears number twenty and plays football for the John Tyler Lions."

Conroe led Tyler 7–3 in that game. With nine minutes remaining, the Lions took possession of the ball on their own 27-yard line.

"They started giving Campbell the ball on every play," remembers coach Stapler. "We finally caught 'em in a third and nine situation, and you know what Earl did? He threw a pass to the quarterback for a first down! On a 13-play drive, he carried ten times and threw one pass. When they got near the goal, we couldn't hold him. From the five, he carried my whole team into the end zone."

After that, "Superman" wasn't the only name they were calling Earl. The press called him "the Tyler Rose" from that day on.

5 / *The Tyler Rose Is Not for Sale*

People were reading about Earl, all right. He was making headlines every week. Even before No. 20 made *Parade* magazine's All-American Team and the Associated Press All-State first team, the entire state of Texas was talking about its favorite son.

In flash-fire fashion, stories spread about the Tyler Rose. And no one had to ask where Earl picked up the nickname. More than 250 college football scouts traveled hundreds of miles to see Earl run and to see game films of his past runs. Many of them were awed. They'd never seen a high school running back who combined size, strength, and speed as well as Earl Campbell.

Soon, recruiters from major colleges and universities, armed with a flood of scholarship offers, came through the piney woods and knocked on Earl's rickety door. Earl knew his home didn't look "like much to somebody coming in." But to him it was the world. He felt no need to apologize for how or where he lived.

"We don't have much, but we're happy with what

we've got," he once told a reporter. "I'm happy and I'm loved. That's all I want. Without love, you're nobody."

To those who came to Tyler, it mattered not where Earl lived. They would have gladly crisscrossed the nation to find him. What did matter was that each recruiter was hoping to land Campbell and build a winning team around him. Of course, Earl listened politely to their pitches. College was the route toward a pro career. Also, he was grateful that he was getting a chance to go to college—something that probably wouldn't have been possible if the charts didn't indicate that he stood alone as the best high school ball carrier in Texas.

Texas University head coach Darrell Royal was among the most noted recruiters Earl met. Royal had a keen eye for talent and an extra sense about a player's desire and attitude. Over the past twenty years, he had made UT famous as the top football school in the state—*the* team to upset in the Southwest Conference and, frequently, in the nation. Normally, Royal didn't believe that if he wanted a job done right, he had to do it himself. But this case was different. Now, he came bouncing down the highway, past the junkyard, and up the dirt driveway to the Campbells' home. The coach was barely seated on the couch in a small, sparsely furnished room, when Earl asked him outright about something he had to know. "Coach Royal, I heard you don't like black people," said Earl. Then he waited for a reply. When Royal denied the charge, Earl believed he had spoken the truth.

Coach Royal told Earl that he was raised on a farm in Oklahoma, much like the Campbells' home, and that he did his share of chores, even though he didn't particularly care for farm life. He said that his grandmama had taken

16

care of him. "But she died before I could do anything for her," the coach said sadly.

Those words hit hard. Earl made up his mind right then that someday he'd repay his mother for all she'd done for him.

The Longhorn coach spent three hours talking about football and trying to convince Earl and his mama that the University of Texas was the place to be. Royal was unaware that Earl's first college choice at that moment was Houston. His father's family came from there. And although his size and speed suggested he'd be an ideal UT Wishbone fullback, he preferred running at tailback in Tyler and Houston's Veer formation. The Veer is different from the Wishbone in that it has an extra receiver and two running backs instead of three.

At the time, what Coach Royal did know was that the prized schoolboy was being offered something extra by several schools. Many who should have known better would have done anything to get Earl. Nevertheless, when Royal brought up the subject of extra attractions, commonly called "inducements," Earl was not shy about stopping the coach. He would not be bribed. "My people were bought and sold when they didn't have a choice," said Earl, so matter-of-factly that the words raised goose bumps on the coach's skin. "Earl Campbell is not for sale."

Money didn't excite Earl. He didn't have a car, and he didn't really yearn for one. He cared more about owning an additional pair of jeans and being as fine a runner as Jimmy Brown. His main interest lay in what a college or university could do for him. Certainly, no one could blame him for thinking the only way to go was up. For years, he had watched the roses growing from almost nothing. And

17

he'd done a lot of praying in the rose fields. "I always felt like one day the good Lord would let me have my chance," reveals Earl. "I worried about when it was going to come, but I didn't mind waiting." Now, he wouldn't have to wait any longer.

After Coach Royal's visit, Earl told a friend, "I'm going to college for an education first and football second. My goal in life is to build a house for my mother so that when she lies down at night, she can't see the Big Dipper."

After narrowing the field of colleges to Arkansas, Houston, Oklahoma, Baylor, and Texas, Earl made plans to visit the last four. Meanwhile, he was still on Coach Royal's mind. Like all the football powerhouses that were trying to recruit Earl, Royal knew he was a rare talent. Sure, there were other players with flashy statistics around the country, but the Tyler Rose had something else going for him. He was a likable young man with a good head on his shoulders. That in itself had recruiters buzzing. Coach Royal beat a path back to Tyler. He wanted Earl as much as everyone else did, if not more.

Royal felt that Texas's biggest threat was Oklahoma—the last school Earl was to visit. But then, before he went north of the Red River to Norman, Oklahoma, Earl made up his mind: "Coach, I'm coming to Texas," he told Royal, "but I want to visit Oklahoma."

Once Earl committed himself to the Longhorns, Royal suggested that, if his decision was firm, he should cancel his date with Oklahoma. That offended the bluest chip in the state. To Earl's thinking, the coach was questioning his word, and he was not bashful about saying so.

Although Royal heard that Campbell liked what he saw in Oklahoma, he didn't ask Earl about the visit until three years later when the two were sitting together on the bus going to the Oklahoma game.

"Earl, after visiting Oklahoma, if you hadn't given me your word, would you still have come to Texas?" asked Royal.

Earl thought a moment. Then he looked at Royal and said, "Coach, I don't really know."

It meant something to Earl that he had given his word.

6 / *Down and Out*

Earl's decision to accept a four-year full scholarship to the University of Texas didn't surprise many people. After all, top athletes are supposed to go to the top colleges in their sports. But some townspeople did question Earl's ability to do college work. These busybodies said he could never make it at the University of Texas because of his low high school grades. Earl tried not to let their comments bother him. He knew he wasn't an academic genius, but he was intelligent, and he did have a C average in high school. Moreover, he was the first to admit that he had weak study habits and that he hadn't applied himself at John Tyler. Earl knew that college would not be easy. "But the sun doesn't shine every day," he said. Still, at UT he decided he would concentrate on his studies as dutifully as he did on football. And he did. At Texas, he earned mostly B's and C's. Equally important, he missed only six classes in the next four years, as a communications major with the hope of going into broadcasting.

As the fullback in a Wishbone offense, Earl rambled up the middle for 928 yards in his freshman year and romped for a conference-leading 1,118 yards as a sopho-more. Saturday after Saturday, Earl ran with tremendous strength and balance. With his shoulders thrust forward,

Earl and Coach Royal plan ahead. (The Daily Texan staff)

Ann Campbell flashes the University of Texas "Hook 'em Horns" sign. (Black Star)

he extended a powerful stiff arm and decked tacklers who got in his way. Some would-be tacklers didn't realize how fast he was; they'd set a tackle only to have Earl pass right by.

After each game, "I'd bust out of the locker room," says Earl, "and I'd be happy until the time I hit the door. Then I'd feel real sad because I'd see all my friends going off with their fathers.

"It was very hard growing up without a father, and it still is now," Earl confesses. "In college, it was something I had to adjust to."

For his efforts, the big, bruising back was selected two years in a row to be a member of the All-Southwest Conference squad and, as a sophomore, to the Coaches' All-American Team.

As Earl's junior year unfolded, his drive toward a record-shattering collegiate career came to an abrupt halt. After getting off to a sunny start, he pulled a muscle in his left leg. Instead of letting the injury heal by sitting out the following week's game, Earl played.

As it turned out, Earl unconsciously transferred much of his weight to his other leg and put too much pressure on it. Finally, a pulled muscle sidelined him for most of six games and cast a shadow on his future. Clearly, Earl learned a difficult lesson: "Regardless of how high you get, you can always be brought down."

The mighty Tyler Rose suddenly was no more effective than a common dandelion. All he could do was to stand helplessly by as the Texas Longhorns learned how the rest of the world played. Earl was their offense, and he was out. Remarkably, he still led the team in rushing with 653 yards, but his injury had an unsettling effect on the 'Horns. With Earl on the bench, Texas dropped to 5–5–1 in

An unhappy Earl. (Black Star)

a season when the Longhorns had expected to compete for the national championship. Their 1976 record was, in fact, the worst in Darrell Royal's two decades as head coach. As a result, Texas athletic director Darrell Royal cheerlessly replaced himself as head coach of the slumping team. What's more, the Earl Campbell story almost ended.

For years, Earl had been thinking about becoming a professional football player. Now, sitting on the bench, he thought his football career was over. Not only was he filled with pain, but—much worse—with self-pity. However, his roommate and friend, James "Sugar Bear" Yates, would have none of the latter. As storm clouds brewed one nasty day—a day Sugar Bear claims he'll never forget because the shock of what happened nearly "killed" him—Earl came into their room in Jester Center Dormitory. Sugar Bear was studying, concentrating hard. In spite of Earl's size, his roommate insists he didn't notice when Earl walked in. Then Earl voiced his frustration: "Sugar Bear, I'm quitting football," announced Earl. "I'm going to tell Coach Royal that I am."

"What, man?" exclaimed Sugar Bear, jumping up.

"I'm quitting because my name isn't Earl Campbell anymore. It's 'How's-your-leg.' Every day it's 'How's-your-leg,' " Earl said with a groan.

"What made the question all the more painful," he later explained, "was that every day it's all I thought about, anyway."

"Stick it out," Sugar Bear sternly told Earl. "Fans will be fans, but they're behind you all the way, or they wouldn't be so concerned about you."

Yates had been an All-State defensive tackle at Conroe High School and a defensive tackle at Texas before knee problems forced him to quit football during his sophomore year. He became Earl's close friend when the two shared many classes as freshmen. Once, when Earl's alarm clock wasn't working, he asked Sugar Bear if he would mind calling him the next morning to awaken him for their eight o'clock class. Before long, the two were calling each other every day, depending upon who was up first.

One Sunday, Sugar Bear dressed for church. He didn't tell anyone that he went to church. "I didn't know what their reaction would be," he explains.

When the Bear walked out of his door, he spotted Earl in the hall. "Hey, where you goin', man?" asked Sugar Bear.

"To church," replied Earl.

From then on, the pair went together to the Mount Oliver Baptist Church every Sunday.

Just a few days after Earl talked about quitting football, Sugar Bear, Earl, and his twin brothers (who were sophomores at Texas) were leaving church when a young boy gave Earl a small wooden plaque. Earl hung the sign on his dormitory bedroom wall. It read: "Keep me going, Lord."

And He did. Soon, Earl was going strong. In fact, upon hearing that Pittsburgh's Tony Dorsett had won the 1976 Heisman Trophy—college football's most treasured prize, given to the nation's most outstanding college player—Earl said to himself, "Someday *I'm* going to win it."

After that, whenever his old doubts about his future in football returned, he quickly pushed them away. For Earl, "someday" would be in 1977 or never. He had only one year of college eligibility remaining. That meant there was no time for him to be discouraged.

7 / A New Game Plan

When Darrell Royal resigned after successfully coaching the Longhorns for twenty years, Fred Akers unexpectedly succeeded him. This caused much grumbling among Texas boosters. Many influential alumni thought Mike Campbell, Royal's defensive coordinator for more than a decade, should have gotten the job. Thirty-eight-year-old Akers was born on St. Patrick's Day, but, to his knowledge, a shamrock had never won a game for him. What did win games was hard work in Blytheville, Arkansas, where he was the only one of nine children in his family to finish school. Through his tireless efforts, he earned a football scholarship to the University of Arkansas, where he played defensive back and place-kicked. One of his teammates was Barry Switzer, later a coach at Oklahoma. After he graduated, Akers coached in the high school ranks at three Texas schools—in Port Arthur, Edinburg, and Lubbock—before he arrived at the University in 1966. Oddly enough, it was Mike Campbell who recommended him to Royal.

"He was a shiny new dime . . . he had an attractive wife, a good personality and a good football mind," said Royal, who took an immediate liking to Akers and decided he wanted him as an assistant. Akers kept that job for the next nine years until Wyoming lured him away. In the sec-

26

ond year of his two-year stay at Wyoming, he led the Cowboys to the Western Athletic Conference Championship and to a bowl.

Now, he was eager to take the Steers to the top of the football world again. But there were complicating matters at Texas, where the big tower glows orange when the Longhorns win. Akers was in the uncomfortable position of having to prove himself as he began rebuilding UT's image.

"A lot of people left him in the position of proving himself," said a source inside the athletic department. "There were a lot of hard feelings among the Mike Campbell supporters."

Again, ambitious Fred Akers began proving himself through hard work. On spring nights, he worked long and late in his seco..d-floor office at Memorial Stadium.

"There's a lot of talent here," said the new UT boss to an assistant, as he made plans to take advantage of it. "Darrell did a good recruiting job." (In truth, Akers had done some of it himself, but he never even mentioned it.)

Because Coach Akers had been in town to see Earl get started at Texas, he knew what he was inheriting when he returned to the campus. Earl was the Longhorns' hope. Though Earl's durability could no longer be taken for granted, Coach Akers had every intention of making him his major weapon in a championship drive. A good showing by Texas as a team would not only help Akers prove himself, but would also help Earl's chances of picking up college football's most cherished prize. Everyone knew he had been a Heisman Trophy candidate since his sophomore year and that his injury had taken him out of the running as a junior.

After studying many films, Akers put Royal's famed Wishbone offense in a drawer and carefully designed his own Veer and I offenses with scheming variations. Defenses were catching up with the Wishbone, cutting back its effectiveness. The Veer would allow Earl to use his speed and exceptional strength on pitchouts when the quarterback tossed him a quick underhand pass. As a tailback in the I formation, Earl would no longer be confined to banging up the middle as he was when the Wishbone was employed.

Also on the team were two of the finest wide receivers in the country. One was senior split end Alfred Jackson, the other, sophomore flanker Johnny "Lam" Jones, an Olympic sprinter who had won a Gold Medal in Montreal in the 4 x 100 relay. Texas also boasted Russell Erxleben, the nation's leading punter.

Earl, for one, liked the new Veer offense that Akers installed. It meant that he could play a more versatile role. He would be able to utilize more of his speed, and he would have more open-field opportunities. Having confidence would give Earl the strength and daring to make maneuvers that he otherwise might be afraid to try. "I'm going to be working on my confidence this summer," said Earl. He should have added that he would also be working on his weight.

In spring practice, one of the first things Coach Akers did was to suggest that Earl lose some weight. He had played his junior year at a hefty 242 pounds. The coach wanted him to report in for his senior year at 220, believing the lighter weight would improve Earl's performance and make his legs less susceptible to problems. Earl took Akers at his word, happy that his coach had enough interest in him to tell him what to do.

Earl and Alfred Jackson share a joke. (Kit Brooking, Austin-American Statesman)

Actually, after Earl had given Coach Akers's request some thought, he admitted to a friend, "I think that was one problem last year. I got a little too heavy and my legs couldn't take it."

After classes ended in May, Earl stayed in Austin for a summer of work and preparation. He shared an apartment with teammate Alfred Jackson and found two jobs: one in construction, the other making deliveries for a tile company. Both jobs required considerable lifting. To his work load, Earl added 200 to 300 sit-ups a day, racquetball, weight lifting, and running. All the while he dedicated himself to his final season at Texas and to an opportunity to play pro ball. Earl was more determined than ever to spend the next part of his life being paid for playing football. "I've worked for the chances I've had since the fourth grade," he told a reporter. "And I know I am working for my chances now. I don't think I've ever been this hungry for football."

Knowing Earl was at 225 and dieting, Mrs. Campbell didn't worry about fixing his favorite meals during the one week he was in Tyler. She should have known he'd miss them. While he was growing up, she had made him three hot meals a day. Earl vividly recalls his mother's breakfasts: "We always had eggs, homemade biscuits, bacon, and rice. And in the afternoons, we'd have homemade cornbread, red beans, some greens, cabbage, and a glass of buttermilk."

Just thinking about his mama's meals made Earl hungry, especially since she wasn't fixing them. Consequently, one morning, Mrs. Campbell awoke to find this note on the table:

Mama,
Wake me up when you fix breakfast. I need it.
Earl

Finally, the loss of 22 pounds and the knowledge that he'd be running from the Veer and I formations gave Earl the confidence he needed. On the way back to school, he decided that in 1977 he would not settle for one man tackling him. "And I really don't intend for two of 'em to get the job done," he told himself, as he set out to lock horns with the opponents.

8 / *There's No Roping the Longhorns*

The University of Texas was gloomily ranked low on the media's rating list when the 1977 football season began, mainly because of its 1976 record. There seemed little hope of the Longhorns' improving their tarnished image. They would be a young team—starting eleven sophomores, four offensive and seven defensive. In truth, many experts thought a 7–4 prediction for the season *extremely* optimistic. What's more, for the first time in a football-mad state, UT's large and loyal following was talking more about basketball than football. ABC-TV had scratched the Longhorns off national television, and supporters in the Dallas area had dropped the Texas football television coverage.

But, believe it or not, the new Texas coach was almost too busy to notice. He was spending his days building a togetherness approach, preaching oneness and citizenship—knowing that morale is usually down after a disappointing year.

"It sounded like Patton's address to his troops," said someone who overheard Akers.

"If you get a parking ticket, pay it," Coach Akers told

31

his men. "If you don't, you're off the team. . . . Don't say something in front of a girl you wouldn't want to say to your sister," he went on. Then he told them he didn't want to hear any dirty words or salty language either. "Oh, yes, and travel dressed like gentlemen."

Then, surprisingly, he swung open his door to the players, and told them he hoped to be both their friend and their coach. In turn, they welcomed the opportunity to talk with him and appreciated the fact that they could discuss anything. After all, he was no stranger; he had recruited many of them.

Fred Akers also worked with the cheerleaders, the student body, the sophomores, and with Earl Campbell on being the all-around back he wanted to be—one that could run, block, and catch.

Some say that, to keep reporters out of his way, Akers told them, "We are not ready at this point to be a contender."

Joked Leon Fuller, the defensive coordinator, "We're so young, we hold hands going onto the field."

"There is nothing we can't overcome," Akers emphasized to his team behind closed doors. "Nothing."

Three workouts a day convinced the players just how serious the coaches could be. "But nobody complained," said Brad Shearer, senior defensive tackle, who had limped around Austin favoring a leg in 1976. "We all saw the coaches going to work at eight o'clock and not leaving until ten o'clock at night. They were working 14 hours a day to make something happen. We decided we would have one heck of a team if we just worked as hard as the coaches."

"We saw Coach Akers establish a winning program at Wyoming," added offensive guard, Rick Ingraham. "We knew he had something going for him if he could take them from nothing to a bowl. We all dedicated ourselves to being number one."

Led by Earl, Texas crushed Boston College 44–0 in the first game of the season, although the Eastern team had beaten them the year before. Next, they bumped off Virginia 68–0, and Rice 72–15. There was no question about it; in the first three games, Earl looked like nothing less than an outstanding Heisman candidate.

Coach Akers liked throwing on first down, opening things up. And Earl liked running out of the Veer and I— off tackle, around end, through opposing defenses. He was so strong that he could run with tacklers clinging to him. Few could stop him one-on-one.

He was in even better shape than the opposition realized. He had drastically slimmed down his thighs, and he began wearing pantyhose that supported his legs.

Coach Akers had his defense attacking and playing man-for-man coverage in the secondary. Coach Royal had preferred the zone, giving up the short pass and concentrating on preventing the big one. Under Akers, every man was responsible for a man, and the defense was to give away nothing. The new coach's philosophy better suited the players' talents. On defense, Earl's twin brothers and company hated to give up an inch. Nevertheless, the experts who had picked Texas to finish fifth in the Southwest Conference weren't impressed. They said, "Wait until Texas plays Oklahoma." A week later, Texas did.

The Steers stayed in the dressing room, taping their ankles and looking at their pictures in the program rather than listen to "Boomer Sooner," the song of their hated rivals. However, the battle of the un-tied and unbeaten

No. 20, Earl Campbell, leads the way. (Ed Malcik, Austin-American Statesman)

The Texas Longhorns take on the University of Oklahoma in the Cotton Bowl in Dallas. (Jay Godwin, The Daily Texan)

teams could not be avoided for long. To be sure, everyone knew the Longhorns had not defeated the Sooners since 1970. If it was true that history keeps repeating itself, it was only logical that the 'Horns would soon be losers.

"We have a big advantage," Coach Akers told his team, moments before they raced onto the field in front of 72,032 fans. "Oklahoma does not know how good a football team you are."

With that, Akers held his breath as a new Texas play resulted in a turnover. The interception put the ball at the Texas 14 with the showdown just six seconds old.

All week, Earl had worked in secret on a halfback pass, certain the Sooners were lurking behind every blocking sled. Then, when the maneuver was tried on the second offensive play, Oklahoma tackle Dave Judgens intercepted the ball. Luckily for the Orange, fullback Kenny King mishandled the football three plays later for the Sooners' twenty-eighth fumble of the year. At last, Earl was off and running—until Texas ran into trouble. On the Steers' seventh play, quarterback Mark McBath hobbled out of the game. Exactly nine offensive plays later, with the clock still running down in the first quarter, Texas's second-string quarterback, Jon Aune, was carried away. This left the third-team quarterback, Randy McEachern, to engineer a triumph, and Earl to save the day.

"Nervous?" someone asked Randy in the huddle. "Oh, no," he said. "Unless you consider your heart stopping a sign of nervousness."

Quickly, Earl took the pressure off. Running out of the I, he bolted, turned, and high-jumped an OU defender to score the game's only touchdown and put the 'Horns ahead to stay, just before half time, 10–3. Before the afternoon

Earl is mangled by Oklahoma. (The Daily Texan)

Earl takes the pressure off quarterback Randy McEachern. (The Daily Texan)

ended, he rang up 126 yards on 23 carries. This confirmed Oklahoma defensive coach Larry Lacewell's suspicion when he got the word that Texas would run from the I with Campbell at tailback.

"I was afraid they'd do something like this," he said. "At tailback, Campbell will be almost unfair."

Although his teammates were hooting and hollering, Earl was weary after his day on the job. Reporters found him dressing in one corner of the locker room. When he spoke, his voice was slow and deliberate: "No, I wasn't playing for revenge," he said, as the media recorded his words. "I was just out there to play a football game. No, I don't know how many yards I had today, but whatever I had, it was worth it. It's a great thrill playing against a team like Oklahoma. The Longhorn team, though, is the greatest." While putting on a gray pin-striped suit, he volunteered, "What I did out there today, I expected. I've been working real hard in practice to be as good as I can."

Adding the finishing touches to his outfit with blue patent-leather shoes, Earl patiently answered one last question. "No, I haven't given a lot of thought to the Heisman Trophy. I'm a team man. I can't worry about the Heisman and play football at the same time. If it happens, it happens. It would be nice, but it's not the only thing in life."

This was not the time to tell anyone how much he wanted the trophy. Once more, Earl simply refused to talk about Earl.

In Austin, fans came out of the woodwork to greet the Longhorn plane. Many were wearing T-shirts appropriately inscribed, "Campbell is Souper" and "Randy's Dandy."

Earl talks with the press. (Black Star)

When reporters asked the pair what was the biggest thrill of the game, they responded simply, "The end."

Alone in his office, Coach Akers reflected on the high price his team had paid for victory with the loss of its first two quarterbacks. Backing up Randy were three freshmen. Tough, unbeaten Arkansas was next on the schedule. If Earl was to continue to look good, the 'Horns had to look good, Akers knew. A man didn't win the Heisman alone.

Said Akers, "I think we're going to find out what we're made of."

His team did. Arkansas was leading well into the fourth quarter with a mere four minutes showing on the clock when Earl turned a fake, reverse-screen pass into a 27-yard run. Then he continued to drive into a 20-mile-an-hour wind to destroy the Razorbacks 13–9 before the final whistle. The Longhorns knew what they wanted and were impossible to stop.

"Victory comes with oneness," reported Coach Akers. "This team is so unselfish. . . . We were just confident that somehow we would win it!"

"That was great running, Earl," a Texas booster said enthusiastically.

"That's why they call me a running back," Earl smiled.

Some people thought that perhaps Earl should be called "the team," after his most recent Heisman-like performance of 188 yards rushing and 28 yards receiving. His shiftiness accounted for all but 118 yards of Texas's total offense and made Big Earl the top ground gainer in the Southwest Conference with 685 yards—although he wasn't aware of it.

"Oh, really?" asked Campbell later, when the press

pointed this out. "That's great, but when I break records, the offensive line breaks records, too," he said humbly, displaying the modesty that made him an exceptional person. Yet, he hadn't had a particularly satisfying game because he had fumbled the ball. When he was trying to get into position to stiff-arm the defensive backs, they had hit him, and the ball had rolled loose.

Later, Earl more than redeemed himself. Suddenly, the Steers were the toast of the town. "Orangebloods" who had thought all was lost because Mike Campbell wasn't named head coach were talking about a championship again. Moreover, following the Longhorns' 30–14 drubbing of Southern Methodist University the next week, television programmers were juggling their schedules to cover the team. Meanwhile, reporters were claiming they needed the strength of giants plus NFL helmets to enter the Longhorn dressing room. It seemed as if everyone wanted to shake hands with Coach Akers and the team that was soon to be ranked No. 1.

Back in Austin, the Texas victory tower cast its orange glow over the 40-acre campus.

9 / *A Heisman for Earl?*

Suddenly, there was great interest in Austin in the Heisman Trophy. Longhorn fans were asking when it would be awarded, who voted on it, and especially what Earl Campbell's chances were of getting it after he was through rewriting Texas record books.

Over the years, the Heisman Trophy has been given to the nation's most outstanding player. But in 1977, many people were becoming positive it was an award that went to a midwestern or northern running back or quarterback. Since the first Heisman Trophy was awarded in 1935 to Jay Berwanger, a University of Chicago halfback, all but two winners have been either quarterbacks or offensive backs. The only exceptions were ends Larry Kelley of Yale, in 1936, and Leon Hart of Notre Dame, in 1949. No interior lineman had ever won the Heisman, nor had there ever been a Heisman winner in Longhorn football history, which began in 1893. Players from the Southwest Conference rarely won the Heisman. The only Southwest Conference winners were: John David Crow of Texas A&M (1957); Doak Walker of SMU (1948); and Davey O'Brien of TCU (1938).

Traditionally, the recipient was announced at a news conference at the Downtown Athletic Club in New York City on the last Tuesday in November. The annual black-tie Heisman dinner was usually held a week later. However, in 1977, the spokesman for the sponsoring New York Downtown Athletic Club said the announcement would be postponed until December 8, when the winner would be announced in a nationally televised extravaganza at the conclusion of a variety show. Also added to the agenda would be six lesser awards: best offensive end, best offensive lineman, best offensive back, best defensive lineman, best defensive back, and best linebacker.

At one time, approximately 1,300 sportswriters and sportscasters were eligible to vote for the nation's top college football player. But during 1977, the Heisman Memorial Trophy Committee reviewed voting procedures and both scissored and restructured the number of electors in each region. This meant that approximately 1,050 members of the media would be casting votes in 1977.

Nonetheless, Earl's chances of getting the award were seemingly good. Oklahoma State's Terry Miller, the preseason favorite, was thought to be his toughest competition. He was a two-time Associated Press All-American, and he had finished fourth in the Heisman voting in 1976. But Oklahoma State was not having its best season. Although the award is an individual one, a team's record is also taken into consideration because one measure of an individual's performance is what he contributes to his team. In this case, if Earl and Terry split the voting in the Southwest section, a third candidate's chance of winning would increase. Those in the running were quarterbacks Guy Benjamin of Stanford, Rick Leach of Michigan, and

Doug Williams of Grambling; three time All-American tight end Ken MacAfee; and his Notre Dame teammate Ross Browner, a defensive end and the winner of the 1976 Outland Trophy as the nation's top lineman.

Still, Earl's chances weren't hurt when *The Football News* projected him the winner.

10 / *Earl Keeps*
Texas on Top

Although former coach Royal had persuaded him to come to Texas, Earl's finest moments as a college football player occurred after Coach Akers junked Royal's Wishbone offense in favor of the Veer and I formations. Game after game, Earl was being hit, but not stopped. By the clipboard count of Coach Akers's official bookkeeper, assistant coach Richard Ritchie, Earl was getting more than half of his yards after contact with the opposition. In the season's seven games, 704 of his 1,015 yards came after breaking tackles. These figures were being kept "to emphasize you need to do some things on your own," reported Coach Akers. "Some backs run only as far as you block 'em," he told sportswriters. "If you block six yards' worth, that's what they make." But not Earl, the player his teammates simply called "the Man."

CAMPBELL'S "HIT AND RUNS"

OPPONENT	Yards Before Hit	Yards After Hit	Total
Boston College	39	48	87
Virginia	58	98	156
Rice	103	28	131
Oklahoma	10	114	124
Arkansas	67	121	188
SMU	29	184	213
Texas Tech	5	11?	116
Totals	311	704	1,015

The Longhorns were having their troubles holding onto a slim 14–13 lead until Earl took over and extinguished the spirit of the Houston Cougars before 72,124 Houstonians, the largest Cougar crowd ever.

Earl had been in bed the night before the game with a sore throat and fever. But there wasn't time to dwell on it. In spite of feeling weak, he opened the third quarter with a 43-yard touchdown sprint and followed with a 40-yard gain that set up more of the same. Finally, he wound up with 173 yards on 24 carries, and UT ended up with a 35–21 victory.

Earl was getting better each game. With a fourth-string quarterback at the helm—because all the rest were injured—and with the pressure on Earl's wide shoulders, the No. 1 Longhorns rolled past TCU 44–14. Next, on national television the Steers trapped the visiting Baylor Bears in another UT melodrama, 29–7. Earl's scoring bolts pushed his game total to 181 yards for 30 carries.

"Earl Campbell is super," said Corky Nelson, Baylor defensive coordinator and former Tyler High coach. "We tried to stop him every way we could."

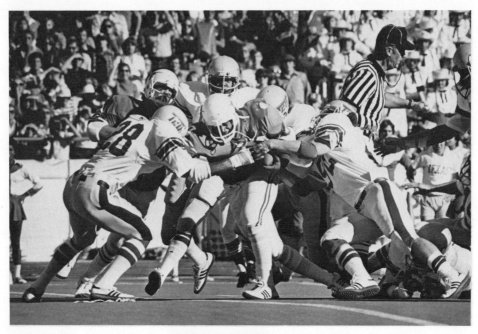

Unstoppable Earl keeps rolling along past Texas Christian. (Austin-American Statesman)

Earl selects some soul music. (Black Star)

Added linebacker Jerry Harrison, "He's the best back we've faced all year."

The Texas defense stood out, too. Said Baylor halfback David Seaborn, "Every time I turned around, Shearer was there. And Tim Campbell* is the hardest guy I've had to block on this year. Their defense is the best we've seen this year."

Now all that stood in the way of a perfect season and a Cotton Bowl berth was Texas A&M. (The Longhorns had an annual invitation to the post-season classic every year from 1969 to 1974 before falling into sad times.)

Earl was prepared to make his final game in a Texas jersey his finest. The evening before the Aggie game, he locked his dorm room door, took his telephone off the hook (he had never bothered to get an unlisted number), put some soul music on the stereo, and fed his goldfish and catfish. Then he rested until Coach Akers called a meeting to pump up his team. After the coach carried on about what a fine team the Aggies had, how big and how quick they were, and how important this game was, he said, "But gentlemen, it does not have to be close. Good night."

"Never a lazy step," Brad Shearer reminded his teammates in the locker room the next day.

When the Aggie band finished playing, Coach Akers pointed out, "They've already done what they do best—march, hut, and holler. Now we're going out to do what we do best."

A roar went up in the dressing room.

Coach Akers encouraged each player individually be-

---

* Tim Campbell and his twin, Steve, are Earl's brothers.

fore he headed out to the field. "Ricky Churchman, just go out there and be your normal, terrible, nasty, ornery self."

With Earl, the brief conversation was in whispers. "Earl, I really expect 170 yards out of you today," said his coach.

"I'm ready," Earl answered in his usual calm, unhurried voice. And there was no doubt about it, he was ready.

Playing his final game as a Longhorn, Earl barreled for a personal best 222 yards and scored four touchdowns. The Steers won their eleventh straight game 57–28, claimed the Southwest Conference title, and retained the No. 1 ranking in college football.

"How did you get to be so good?" a reported asked the Longhorns' No. 20.

"I don't drill on trying to be the best," he said. "I just expect to be."

"Seldom, if ever, do you exceed your own expectations," Coach Akers had told his players more than once.

"There's only one way to bring down Earl," insisted Aggie linebacker Kevin Monk after his team lost. "Grab hold and hope for help."

Longhorn Glenn Blackwood marveled: "I've never seen a guy who wants that extra half yard so badly. Every time."

For Texans who like their runs long, Earl was king of the earth. He topped the nation in rushing with 1,744 yards and won the national scoring title with 114 points. He also finished first in all-purpose running with 1,855 yards. Statistics showed that he had gained 1,054 of his yards after he slipped and ripped away from at least one would-be

Earl changes into his ninetieth tear-away jersey of the season. (Black Star)

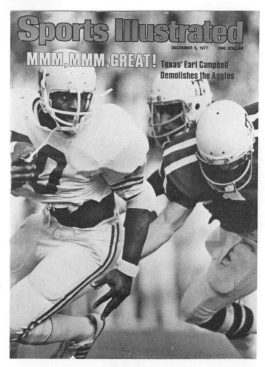

"Souper" Campbell is featured on the cover of Sports Illustrated. (Austin-American Statesman)

tackler. Equally important, Earl finished the season with 267 carries, an average of 6.53 per run.*

In four years, he collected 4,443 yards, a conference and school career record, despite working for three years in the Wishbone, where the big chunks of yardage come less often. And despite sharing the fullbacking spot with Roosevelt Leaks his freshman year, and despite his being hurt as a junior and not playing up to his potential, having played only two 100-yard games. At the University of Texas, Earl also set records: the most touchdowns in a football season (19); the most career touchdowns (41); the most points in a career (246); and the most touchdowns in a single game (4) on two occasions.

"If he doesn't win the Heisman, they ought to throw the things away," Coach Akers firmly asserted. "Earl represents what that trophy is all about. It's not just an athletic thing. . . . You better believe he's a sensational human being."

---

* Tony Dorsett had set the record for backs with over 300 carries by averaging 5.76 yards on 338 totes for 1,948 yards in 1976. But even if the statisticians added 35 no-gainers to Earl's figures, bringing his carries up to 302, his average of 5.77 would still take the title away from Tony.

11 / *Who Else but Earl?*

As far as Coach Akers and University of Texas athletic director Darrell Royal were concerned it was truly impossible to even imagine anyone but Earl winning the Heisman Trophy.

"Earl's performance speaks for itself. It's evidence enough of what a great football player he is," former coach Royal told reporters. Conceding that he might be prejudiced, Royal was more than willing to talk about the Longhorn he considered a rare gem. After all, Earl was one of his favorite people. "The good Lord gave Earl a great physique and an instinct you don't learn," Royal said. "You can't teach a player to run fast, to run powerfully, or to make the right cuts when a hole closes. Furthermore, he's every bit as exceptional off the field as on the field. He's a deeply religious man, a kind man. He's not perfect, and he never has claimed to be, but he's honest, patient, and a hard worker. I give an A plus to Campbell the man. He deserves every bit of credit he gets. He's the greatest Longhorn ever and certainly the greatest player I've seen in my career."

But although the coaches believed Earl's name should be on every Heisman ballot, that didn't necessarily mean the rest of the country felt the same way. It was rumored that some people on the East Coast just plain didn't like Texas—neither the university nor the state. Not only sportswriters and sportscasters, but other media people, too. It seemed to those who lived in the state that whenever Texans were portrayed on television, they were usually straight-shooting, tough-talking people with strange accents and lots of money and idle time. For this reason, the Southwest felt it was doubtful that Earl would be the pick of the East.

Nonetheless, when the calculators stopped calculating, it was Earl who led the nation in rushing,* although he carried the ball 44 fewer times than running back Charles Alexander of LSU, and 47 fewer times than Terry Miller, who stood second and third respectively in yardage.

It was common knowledge that the Steers' offense was built around Earl. And that would help him because of the firm conviction that what a player contributes to his team is important. One couldn't help noting that Earl's rushing and scoring efforts helped make Texas the only perfect-record team in the country. He was unstoppable once he began rolling. In fact, in the Longhorns' sternest tests, Earl had his most productive days on the ground, ripping off gains of 124 yards against Oklahoma, 188 yards against Arkansas, 173 yards against Houston, and his career high of 222 yards against the Aggies.

* Earl was the third heaviest rushing champion in NCAA history— outweighed only by Mark Keller, a back for Northern Illinois at 232 pounds in 1973, and Ray McDonald, Idaho, 240 pounds in 1966.

"I still don't know what this Heisman business is really all about," confessed Ann Campbell, who was getting used to reporters stopping by her ,Lhome. "People ask me about it, and I'll tell you what I tell everybody else," she said. "If Earl gets it, then that's nice because it would be quite an honor. But if he doesn't, then being runner-up would be nice, too. It's an honor just to be a contender. I just hope it's given in the right spirit."

Mrs. Campbell wasn't the only person who didn't know what the trophy was all about. Though many are aware that it is awarded annually to the top college football player in the United States, few know much about the man whose name is etched on it.

John William Heisman was born in Cleveland, Ohio, in 1869. He coached football at eight different schools from 1892 to 1929, but his greatest fame was earned at Georgia Tech, where his team five times scored more than 100 points in a game. In 1915, the largest engineering school in the South set the scoring record with a 222–0 win over a pickup Cumberland College team. But before that, while scouting a game between Georgia and North Carolina in 1895, Heisman saw something that gave him an idea. It was an illegal pass, which he soon led a campaign to legalize. Today, John Heisman is called "the Father of the Forward Pass." He is also credited with introducing the center snap, interference on end runs, hidden ball play, the statistical scoreboard, and the quarterback's hike. He is in football's Hall of Fame. At the time of his death in 1936, Heisman was serving as Director of Athletics at the New York Downtown Athletic Club, where the idea of the nation's top football player award was dreamed up in 1935. That same year, it was presented to Jay Berwanger. It wasn't until the following year, after Heisman died, that it was named in his honor.

At nine o'clock on Tuesday morning, December 6, 1977, the New York accounting firm of Harris, Kerr, Forster & Company began secretly counting the 1,050 Heisman ballots of the coast to coast media.

Afterwards, seventeen telephone calls* were made, and the three top contenders for each of the six Downtown Athletic Club awards were invited to fly to New York. The Heisman Trophy winner was among that group.

Bill Little, assistant sports information director at the University of Texas, had the job of tracking down Earl and defensive lineman Brad Shearer to let them know they were among the final candidates. (Both were in San Diego, California, picking up Kodak All-American honors and later taping the upcoming "Bob Hope Christmas Show" in Los Angeles. It was doubtful that Earl even knew he had just been named United Press International Back of the Year. What he did know was that he was an Associated Press All-American.)

The winner of each honor was a closely guarded secret. Only the accountants knew who the winners were for sure. Everyone else would learn their identity at the ceremonies which would be televised live from the Grand Ballroom of the New York Hilton Hotel on Thursday, December 8.

More likely than not, the name of Earl Campbell would be in the secret envelope, Henry Bell, Jr., president

---

* Notre Dame's Ken MacAfee was a candidate for both best offensive lineman and best offensive end.

of Citizens First National Bank in Tyler, believed. He thought it only fitting that Earl's mama be at the ceremonies in New York. Ann Campbell had been the Bells' maid ever since she was pregnant with Earl. Therefore, Mr. Bell wanted to pay her way to the city. Bell decided that he and his wife should go to the ceremonies, too. And not to be left behind were Darrell Royal and his successor, Fred Akers.

12 / *Big Earl's Big Night*

"Actually, I'm just in New York for some kind of function," joked Earl, when being interviewed by a vast throng of reporters before the banquet.

Then, no longer wanting to belittle the trophy's importance, he added, "This is probably the biggest night of my life. If I win the Heisman, it will be a dream come true. Before I take my uniform off, I want to be known as one of those guys who played his position and was one of the best. But no matter what happens tonight, I know there will be a tomorrow."

In his room at the Downtown Athletic Club, where he was staying, Earl was asked the same questions so many times that it would have been understandable if he had bristled. That wasn't his style, though. The closest he had ever come to being upset was during his injury-plagued junior year. Those who had watched Earl play junior high, high school, and college football would be the first to testify that they had never seen him lose his temper, throw a football in anger, or show irritation toward opposing players, officials, or anybody else. Now the easy-going Texan patiently repeated the same answers and responded to the same difficult questions forthrightly.

"What kind of person do you consider yourself to be?" one reporter asked. Earl paused, then slowly said, "I play football when I have my suit on. When I don't, I take care of my other business." Then he added, "I'm 22 years old, and I don't know anyone in this world that I hate, and I don't think anyone hates me. I'm not a football player that brags. All I do is play. People that are interested in football will know what I do. Millions of Japanese won't know what I do, no matter what. Football isn't the only thing. I enjoy making other people happy."

Before long, there was a question about his race. "I don't see Earl Campbell as a black man," he said with no edge to his voice. "I see Earl Campbell as a man. I have too much stuff going on to be drilling on the black and white issue."

The broadcaster who asked him the question apologized.

"Look here," Earl said, "you didn't offend me. I just have a deep voice. You probably haven't heard me talk before."

Next, the question was "What does the Heisman Trophy really mean to you now that it is only a few hours away?"

"It means twenty-two years of hard work," Earl admitted, "but if I don't win the Heisman, I'm going to smile the same old way and do the same old things and fight a little harder."

"But if you do win the trophy, what will you do with it?" a reporter wanted to know.

"I'd take it to the University of Texas so the city of Austin and the student body could have a chance to see it.

Then I'd take it home and present it to my mother. She's the person I'd like to have it."

Then it was time for Earl to get ready for the banquet. Teammate Rick Ingraham was already decked out in a tuxedo. He had come to New York to lend Earl his support.

"Rick's the guy who always motivates me," explained Earl. "After the Texas A&M game, he told me, 'All I ever wanted was for you to make All-Southwest Conference and win the Heisman Trophy.' "*

"It's in the bag," Rick said, his face breaking into a smile.

"I'll believe it tonight," replied Earl, knowing his teammates wanted him to win the trophy as badly as he did.

In the eastern Texas town of Tyler, a family gathered for an evening of television. But it wasn't "Thursday Night at the Movies" they were standing by for. It was CBS's Heisman presentation. Earl's brothers, sisters, relatives, and friends were waiting to see who would carry off the Trophy.

So was the whole state of Texas, as well as the rest of the nation.

Wearing a black dress and smiling, Ann Campbell entered the biggest ballroom she had ever seen. Like an in-

---

* Actually, six Texas Longhorns were named to the UPI All-Southwest Conference team: Earl, his brother Tim, defensive tackle Brad Shearer, defensive back Johnnie Johnson, kicker Russell Erxleben, and offensive guard Rich Ingraham.

ternational airfield, it sparkled with silver and lights. But Mrs. Campbell felt right at home; she was rapidly adjusting to her son's celebrity.

After a lavish dinner in the luxurious hotel, the Downtown Athletic Club presented six preliminary awards to Ken MacAfee of Notre Dame, best offensive end; Ross Browner of Notre Dame, best defensive lineman; Zac Henderson of Oklahoma, best defensive back; Jerry Robinson of UCLA, best linebacker; Chris Ward of Ohio State, best offensive lineman; and Earl Campbell of the University of Texas, best offensive back.

The best offensive back smiled, rose, cleared his throat, and spoke: "I'd like to thank the guys who helped me get this. The guys mainly responsible for my being here are my offensive linemen and all my teammates and our coaching staff. I don't have words to express what they have done for me. They have made me the man that I am today."

Finally, at long last, it was time for football's greatest honor. Thousands of miles away, a roomful of people erupted in cheers as the second Jay Berwanger uttered, "Earl." They were crying, dancing, embracing each other, as their brother walked from his table to the spotlighted podium where he accepted the Heisman Trophy.

"Everybody has dreams," said Earl. "And for me this year has been a dream come true. I hope I can represent what the Heisman Trophy stands for. I will do everything I can toward that aim." His words meant that the world could count on it.

Typically, Earl gave praise to God, his widowed mother, and his teammates for making it all possible. Then he was at a loss for words.

Earl's brothers and sisters listen to his acceptance speech after he is named "Best Offensive Back." (Tyler-Courier-Times-Telegraph)

The House that Earl Built for his mama. (Tyler-Courier-Times-Telegraph)

"When I was a kid and in trouble, I used to say, 'Mama, I'm in trouble,' " he said.

Pausing, he looked toward his mother and added, "So, Mama, I'm in trouble. I don't know what to say." Earl's mother smiled as the 1,500 people attending the dinner laughed in appreciation. Then they burst into thunderous applause and gave a standing ovation to both mother and son.

Well-wishers soon descended upon Mrs. Campbell and the eleven other Tylerites who had made the trip to New York.

"I'm very happy and very proud," said Mrs. Campbell, her eyes glistening with tears. "I had no idea Earl would be the winner."

"You don't find an Earl Campbell on every field or see one every year," said the Longhorn coach. "He is every bit as good a person as he is an athlete. He's solid. He has a tremendous set of values. He has handled success very well. I'm extremely proud of Earl, his family, and our team."

The great Longhorn back, who was wearing a tuxedo with a yellow rose pinned to the lapel, was mobbed by photographers, newsmen, and other people.

"I can't tell you how happy I am," Earl told them. "I'm too happy to cry and too happy to smile. But, yes, I think I deserved the Heisman Trophy because I worked so hard for it. If you had seen how hard I worked for it, you would say, 'Earl, you deserve it.' "

Asked if he had dreamed of winning the prestigious award prior to his outstanding senior season, Earl smiled.

"When I was injured my junior year, I remember sitting in the training room and hearing that Tony Dorsett

A happy moment. Earl gets a kiss from his mother while keeping one hand on his Heisman Trophy. (Wide World Photos)

had won the Heisman," he recalled. "I told myself, 'I'm going to win it.' I'm glad we got out of the Wishbone and into the Bear because it was very helpful to me."

Now, it was on to a pro football career for certain. With the Heisman in hand, Earl could expect to be chosen in the first round of the National Football League draft and to earn more money than most people dreamed of. He said he would spend part of his pro money, when he got it, on a new house for his mother. And the house would have a roof that didn't leak.

"I think that when somebody does what my mother has done, she should be put on a throne and called a queen. I'm going to do everything in my power to see that the remainder of my mother's days will be the happiest days of her life. If you ever loved anybody so much that when you talk about them it gives you tingles inside, well, that's the way I feel about my mama."

"Why do you talk about your mother so much?" Earl had once been asked.

"One reason is that she's so great, and another is that I believe if you are going to let anyone know how you feel about them, don't wait until they die. Always give them roses while they are alive, so they can smell them," he replied.

Earl seemed surprised when somebody asked where he would build the house for his mother. "Why, in the same place," he answered. Then, methodically pursuing one goal at a time, he announced, "Someday, when the greatest football players of all time are discussed, I would like my name to be mentioned. But I know it won't be just by saying it. I'm going to have to work for it. And I'm going to do it."

13 / *The Earl of Texas*

In Austin, the 27-story University of Texas tower blazed orange. A ten-story numeral 1, in honor of Earl, flashed white in the black sky. Cheering students poured from their dormitories. Football fans flooded the streets. Horns honked. Moments after the Heisman Trophy winner was announced in the Big Apple, Earl Campbell's friends and fans began celebrating. Some UT students climbed street lights to wave "Hook 'em Horns" over Guadalupe Street— "the drag" at the edge of campus. And someone painted the name "Earl" on the windshields of cars.

As far as Earl's teammates were concerned, the media voters couldn't have made a wiser choice.

"He's the finest running back I've ever seen," bellowed linebacker Morgan Copeland. "I think he'll go down being recognized as one of the all-time great players."

"It's great," yelled center Wes Hubert. "I knew he was the best!"

"Did you see Ingraham?" asked defensive tackle Allen Rickman. "He was hollering and yelling!"

Although Earl had been quick to give credit to his

teammates for his accomplishment, two Longhorn linemen wouldn't accept it. Tackle George James said, "He did it on his own. Just look at the numbers and how many yards he gained after he was hit."

"It's his," Wes Hubert insisted. "He deserves it. We did what we were supposed to do."

Sugar Bear Yates said Earl didn't know what to expect. "I would watch him go for that extra yard and ask myself, why is he taking those licks?" Yates said. "Then it struck me. He was thinking about a pro contract and building his mama a house."

Earl spent part of the next day on the telephone with his teammates and his girl friend, Tyler nurse Ruena Smith—the same girl friend he has had since he was in the ninth grade.

The "Earl of Texas" was up early the morning after winning the Heisman for a televised appearance on "The Today Show." However, before going to the NBC studios, he stopped in the Athletic Club's coffee shop, where he was offered breakfast, compliments of the cook. Because he was on a tight schedule, Earl politely refused, but promised the cook he'd be back to finish their conversation. Later, Earl took the cook out to breakfast so that they could talk without interruption.

"Half the people in New York wanted to breakfast with Earl this morning," said UT assistant athletic director Bill Ellington, "and he did that!"

That was the way Earl was, and everybody, including the assistant athletic director knew it. Long ago he had learned to make others feel important by being friendly and courteous. Never did he get carried away by self-

The University of Texas tower glows in honor of Earl. (Wide World Photos)

Earl and Ruena Smith. (Black Star)

importance, which is one reason he was so well-liked. Always he was the same old Earl, determined that nothing would change him.

By now, the same old Earl was in the same tuxedo. He and his coach were on their way to the nation's capital where they were to be honored by the Washington Pigskin Club. A club founded by Charles B. Fisher, a black doctor who believed that racial discrimination should not enter athletics. On this, the club's fortieth anniversary, Earl was named Offensive Player of the Year. Ross Browner was named Top Defensive Player, and Fred Akers was designated Coach of the Year.

In one season, Coach Akers had done something few thought could be done. "The whole coaching staff can stick out their chests about this," drawled the man who had returned Texas to the glory it had once known. "It's always nice to be rewarded through recognition."

Still, for two nights in a row, it was Earl who stole the show. He spoke to the high school athletes in the audience, who were anxious to learn his formula for success.

"You have to scratch when it's fourth-and-one," he told his listeners. "You have to scratch at 7 A.M., when it's class time and you don't want to go. Nothing is worth having in this world if it's easy."

Then Coach Akers and Earl returned to the business at hand—their New Year's meeting with Notre Dame in the Cotton Bowl.

14 / *Earl Is Busy*

Again, Earl was the center of attention—this time at the Texas Football Awards presentation, when the fifth leading ground gainer in major college history was named the most valuable player for 1977 by his teammates.

"How's it going?" asked an old acquaintance attending the banquet.

"Fine," answered Earl, as he continued signing autographs. "I just haven't found a short way to spell Campbell yet."

Earl said he was looking forward to finishing school and that he was working out a little. "I hope to play football for a few more years. Maybe somebody will think I'm good enough to pick me up," he added with a wink.

Little did he know that at that very moment a scramble for Campbell was taking place among the NFL's twenty-eight teams. Indeed, there wasn't one club that wouldn't be happy to have him. Never before had a player generated such excitement in the pros.

But Earl hesitated to say which professional team he would prefer to play for, accepting the fact that he had no control over who drafted him or where he'd be living in the fall.

"My favorite team is the Texas Longhorns," he said, skirting the issue.

Earl zeroed in on his best moment at Texas as the game in which the Steers demolished the Aggies. His worst? "Any time it's third and two and they give me the ball."

People were forgetting that Earl had to go to school. He was invited to spend a week in the Bahamas in ABC's Superstar competition—competing against twelve professional athletes and to speak from coast to coast. One lady even asked him to judge a cake-decorating contest. But Earl was going home, and nothing would stand in his way.

Nor would chilly weather and soggy skies prevent 5,000 Tylerites from giving a warm welcome to their Tyler Rose. Everyone cheered as Earl, his mother, and his girl friend rode in an open car through the downtown streets. In the parade in his honor, Earl was joined by Coach and Mrs. Akers, Darrell and Mrs. Royal, and several Tyler dignitaries who were happy to be part of Earl Campbell Appreciation Day.

"People tell me all the time, 'Hey, Earl, you put Tyler on the map,'" Campbell told a crowd in front of the Fountain Place in the center of town. "But there's one thing they're forgetting . . . that you people put me on the map."

Earl then centered his attention on the children in the audience, telling them that not everyone can be a football player like Earl Campbell. "I know I can't be a football player like O. J. Simpson," he said matter-of-factly. "My goal is to do my best and to do what I know is right."

As Earl's fans dined, with the Heisman Trophy as part

Earl with three of his coaches. Left to right: Corky Nelson, Laurence LaCroix, and Fred Akers. (Tyler-Courier-Times-Telegraph)

of the decorations, he signed autographs and talked with old friends. He didn't sit down until a film of his UT football career was about to be shown. Afterward, there were the speakers. Laurence LaCroix was only one of several to praise Earl for his accomplishments. The coach remembered Earl as more than just a talented athlete. He recalled an unassuming lad with a big goal and the willingness to work for it.

As a finale to the day-long celebration, Tyler Mayor Bob Noll and Dr. Earl Christian Kinzie presented Earl with a gift from the townspeople—a brand new green-and-white Ford van, outfitted with carpeting, speakers, a refrigerator, and tables. An inconspicuous nameplate boasted, "Custom-built for Earl Campbell," and the license plate read: RBC 20.

Earl couldn't have been more thrilled. Upon receiving the van, he said, "You people took a guy and made a whole lot of him. You loved me and pushed me. I love y'all and I thank you so much."

As Earl was leaving the banquet, someone asked him what the license plate letters meant. "Running Back Campbell, I guess," he replied. Then he added with just a trace of a smile, "Hey, when somebody gives you something, you don't ask a lot of questions."

15 / Campbell Heads for Houston

The news swept across the city of 2.8 million people as fast as Earl ran through opposing defenses. At last, Houston had him! In what the Oilers' general manager and head coach, O. A. "Bum" Phillips, termed "a commitment to excellence," Houston announced that—after much trouble— they had obtained Tampa Bay's No. 1 draft choice rights. And, in the same breath, they declared they would select Heisman Trophy winner Earl Campbell when the National Football League draft began in eight short days.

There would be no dillydallying. Of the 335 college players in the draft, Earl would be the first to go. He was the man the Oilers wanted. The club wouldn't need the fifteen minutes allotted to each team in the first two rounds to make up its mind. Bum Phillips had decided he wanted the All-American fullback years ago. In fact, the first time Phillips saw a film of Earl bruising tacklers in 1975, the year he became the Oilers' coach, he knew he wanted him on his team.

"Texans hate to lose their college football players more than they do their oil," said Phillips, who has a reputation for taking a straightforward approach to life. "I didn't want the fans anywhere else to claim that Earl was theirs."

No longer would they have a chance.

Earl learned of his future assignment as a professional football player as he was strolling across the Texas campus on April 24, 1977.

"You're destined to become an Oiler," shouted Alfred Jackson, when he finally found his roommate. "Houston just phoned. They're going to make you their first choice!"

"Great! I'm real pleased," said Earl. He then admitted for the first time, "I wanted to stay in Texas and play close to home. A lot of people don't get the chance to play close to home their entire career. I feel real fortunate to do so."

By his own admission, Earl felt about 900 pounds lighter after Houston acquired him. He'd been worried— not only about passing his courses in government, sociology, and Middle Eastern Studies, but also about where he'd be playing ball. Now, his future looked bright as he hurried off to a three o'clock class.

The press was waiting when he came out. One reporter was surprised that Earl would even think of attending a lecture on this big day.

"I go to class, man," said Earl. "I owe this university a lot more than it owes me."

Minutes later, he was telling everyone how delighted he was to be picked up by Houston.

"The Oilers look like a promising team," he said. "Last year [1977] they had a lot of bad breaks and injuries go against them. If it hadn't been for that, they would have made the playoffs. I just hope I can make a contribution and help them make the playoffs. I feel like I can." Then

Earl added, "You know, man, the Oilers' season this past year reminds me of my junior year—frustrating."

Houston finished the 1977 season with eight wins and six losses. While some clubs were already established, Houston was still trying to get there. During the last ten painful years, the Oilers compiled a regrettable 52–84–4 record. Never had they won a division championship, nor had they reached the playoffs since 1969. As a result, the owner of the Oilers, K. S. "Bud" Adams, was looking for ways to improve his team—even if it meant he had to spend some money.

Asked how much money he thought he would get for signing with the Oilers, Earl said he didn't want to talk contract dollars. "If it was up to me, I'd play for $50. But I'm going to leave the negotiations to my agent and my lawyer."

Earl had chosen Mike Trope of Los Angeles as his agent. Trope's clients included every Heisman Trophy winner for the previous six years except John Cappelleti.

As it was, the Oilers wasted no time contacting Trope with the hopes of working out an agreement.

To get Tampa's first pick in the 1978 NFL draft—their prize for finishing with the league's poorest record—the Oilers didn't have to give up the Astrodome or lose Galveston Island, despite rumors to the contrary. But they did have to make a complicated deal with the Buccaneers to be in a position to draft Earl. Warding off interference from the Los Angeles Rams, Houston turned over to Tampa their seventeenth-round No. 1 and 2 choices in the 1978 NFL draft and swapped their No. 3 and 4 picks in 1979 along with quality second-year tight end Jim Giles.

"Jimmy will be an All-Pro in three years," said Oilers' offensive coordinator Ken Shipp. "I wouldn't give him up for anybody less than Earl."

Just having Earl's powerful presence in the backfield made a lot of opponents uncomfortable, and Shipp knew it. "I saw seven films of Earl last year," he said. "Defensive backs hated to see him come through the line. He can break a play, something we have not had."

At UT, Earl was a breakaway threat every time he handled the ball. And, needless to say, Texas gave him plenty of opportunities. Now, all the coaches were hoping that Earl, with his overall speed, would give the Oilers a breakaway threat. That was a dimension their defense had been sorely missing for years.

"But first," Shipp went on, "Earl's got to go to training camp and prove he should be on the field."

In short, Earl had the difficult task of earning a spot in the Oilers' lineup. Being their No. 1 draft choice didn't guarantee success. Some players never reach the heights reasonably or unreasonably expected of them—even Heisman winners. The infamous Heisman Trophy jinx is as celebrated as the *Sports Illustrated* cover curse. A black cloud seems to follow both.

Only time would tell how good a deal the Oilers had made and what the return would be on their investment. Although some people in the front office seemed worried, Coach Phillips believed the outlook was excellent. Asked how long he anticipated it would take for Earl to contribute to his team, Bum said, "About a day or so, as soon as we hand him the ball the first time."

The players, too, were excited about having Earl join their squad. "A hell of a trade," said Carl Mauck, Houston center and self-appointed team spokesman. "We don't know what this kid can do in the NFL, but all of us know what we think he can do. And from what we think he can do, this must be the best Oiler trade since the club acquired Carl Mauck!"

Above the cheers he added, "The guy showed me how tough he was in the Cotton Bowl." (Against Notre Dame, Earl wrung out his 100 yards although Texas lost the national championship.) "He never quit. Every yard he gained was a tough yard. The kind of yard he'll have to gain in the NFL.

"I like Campbell's attitude," said Mauck. "In every interview I've heard him give, he praises his coaches and gives credit to his teammates. He shows a lot of character."

It came as no surprise to anyone that the Oilers selected Earl Campbell when the first day of the draft finally arrived. However, no one anticipated it would be Earl's mother who would announce Houston's choice. "I will make the selection for the Houston Oilers," said Mrs. Campbell, who had been flown to the city by the Houston Sportswriters and Sportscasters Association. "I select my son, Earl Campbell, the best running back in the nation!"

As Bud Adams presented Ann Campbell with a dozen red roses, she added softly, "He's just a little country boy who grew up in the sand in Tyler, and better named the Tyler Rose."

With that, oil-rich Houston's fanatical football followers went wild! Normally calm and composed people were most impatient to get going. Indeed, all that remained to be done was to sign the record-setting running back from Texas. Adams knew Earl wouldn't come cheaply.

The morning of the draft, Campbell was at draft

headquarters in New York after having appeared on "The Today Show." By afternoon, he was airborne for Houston, where the very sight of him stopped traffic. Some fancy footwork on the part of Mike Trope, during twenty hours of intense negotiations, had turned Earl into a millionaire in one incredible day.

The year before, Trope had negotiated a 1.2 million dollar agreement for Tony Dorsett with the Dallas Cowboys. Now, Earl signed a reported 1.34 million dollar six-year pact with a payout extended over a period of twenty years. No doubt about it, the Oilers gained more than an extra point on the Dallas Cowboys, their strongest rival. In landing Earl, Houston got a fellow Texan with a fan club of his own.

When the Oiler season ticket office opened the day after Earl was signed, people were standing in line. In the first hour, 69 tickets were sold—the most ever sold in sixty minutes—in a city where ticket sales had never been overwhelming.

Now, fans were pouring from the side streets onto Fannin Street and into the Oiler box office. During 1977, there were 29,500 season tickets sold. By July 1978, sales were at a record high: 40,327. And by the day of the first game, the 50,153-seat Astrodome was sold out. The influence of Earl, translated into dollars and cents at 111 dollars a season ticket, added up to more than 2 million dollars. Consequently the Texas State network, which carries Houston's games, expanded its market from seven stations to sixty-six.

Understandably, Houstonians were excited about the prospects of their football team. Few had doubts about what Earl could accomplish. After all, they had watched him fuel Texas through an undefeated season to the Southwest Conference Championship before losing to Notre Dame.

"I'm happy to be in Houston," announced the 5-feet 11-inch gigantic drawing card when he met with the city's press for the first time. "Since I was in the fourth grade, I've wanted to be a professional football player," he said. "Then, like now, I had my heroes." Who? Earl reeled them off as assuredly as a quarterback calling a play. "Jim Brown, O. J. Simpson, Chuck Foreman, Franco Harris, and, of course, now Walter Payton."

Earl wanted to avoid any discussion that might cause controversy—subjects such as how much he would earn, where he would line up, what plays he would run, and what number he would wear. He also steered clear of comparisons with Tony Dorsett and rivalries with any other past or present greats.

"We aren't gonna talk about money," Campbell said, refusing to discuss the matter. "That's not my job. I pay somebody to look out for that." But he did say that money wouldn't change him and that the amount he signed for would be sufficient for him to build his mother a house.

When someone pointed out that Earl's old number— 20—at Tyler High and Texas had been assigned by the Oilers the year before to rookie defensive back Bill Currier, Earl said, "I'm not worried about a number. Just as long as I have one. I don't think that's what slips you through a hole, anyway."

Asked what he thought he'd be doing for the Oilers, Campbell quickly and firmly set the record straight: "I heard on the radio this morning that Earl can do what Earl wants to do. That's not true. I'm going to try to do what Coach Phillips wants me to do."

Bud Adams had said that Campbell might rival Cleveland Brown spectacular Jim Brown's performance, but Earl shunned any comparisons.

"I just try to be Earl Campbell and nobody else," he said. "Jim Brown was Jim Brown. I just try to go out and play like I can. I hope Earl Campbell can be the football player everybody expects him to be, as well as a gentleman."

Not surprisingly, journalists persisted in asking Earl whether there would be any rivalry between him and Dorsett, the 1976 Heisman Trophy winner, and No. 1 pick in that year's draft.

"No," Earl patiently replied. "I don't think that would be good for me."

"Have you met Tony?" reporters wanted to know. "What did he tell you about life in the NFL?"

"Tony told me it's not a very easy transition from college to professional ball," Campbell said, choosing his words carefully. "He said he'd had a few problems, but he thought I could handle it. He said the pace is a lot faster in the pros."

There are many adjustments a rookie must make in his first training camp. For the Heisman Trophy winner, unaccustomed to being second or third, some insist there are even more. But Heisman winner or not, every player must learn a new and often more complicated system of football. In addition, he must again prove himself as a player and as a person to his teammates. Some rookies never make the necessary adjustments. And in a game that is as much mental as physical, this can spell trouble.

Earl is never too busy or too tired to play football. Here, he takes time off from looking for an apartment in Houston. (Ray Keeling)

"I think I can make it," said Earl, as his first press conference ended. And the media, known for skepticism, didn't doubt him. After all, hard work was all Earl knew.

16 / *Basic Training*

Although crowded beaches made it clear that the football season was still light years away, the newest members of the troops of General Bum Phillips, an ex-Marine, reported to San Angelo, Texas, for six weeks of training camp. Under orders, Earl spent his first 48 hours preparing for battle—marching from the meeting room to the lunch room to the examining room, equipment room, and dining room, then back to the meeting room and, finally, to his dormitory room. Then the rookies began two-a-day workouts. They had only eight days to prepare for their clash with Kansas City.

The fast-paced camp was one of the results of the National Football League's 1978 expansion to a 16-game schedule from the traditional 14 games. In the past, there had been six pre-season games. Bum and his staff had used the first four to study personnel, then approached the last two as regular season games. In 1978, there were only four pre-season games scheduled. This meant that the Oilers' coaches had only two games in which to study their players before attempting to put them together in what they hoped would be a winning combination.

By his own admission, Earl was scared when he reported to training camp. Like a new student in school, he didn't know if he would be accepted, especially since he was being paid more than anybody else.

Everyone knew that several veterans, who had already proven their ability, had contracts coming up for renewal. Though they weren't yet at camp, none would be too happy with Earl if the Oiler organization paid one man highly, at the expense of the rest. Or in this case, two men. In recent months, the Oilers had signed quarterback Dan Pastorini, with his strong right arm, to a million-dollar pact. Nevertheless, it's common knowledge that a team doesn't win a championship with just a quarterback and a running back. Consequently, Earl hoped all the players were being paid what they really deserved. Otherwise, he knew he was walking into a situation where there would be a lot of uneasiness.

Like all rookies, Earl was ambitious, but he would consider himself successful only if he achieved his goals: he wanted to help the Oilers in whatever way he could. This meant that he needed to have himself ready to hit the field and go right to work. But mixing with his teammates, fitting in, was Earl's major objective. He wanted to be able to say, "Hey, I'm Earl," to people, and to push football aside when they talked.

Clearly, there were hundreds of people who wanted to talk to him. The press wouldn't leave the heralded fullback alone.

"If people want to talk to me, I'll talk to them," said Earl, knowing it was part of his job. But he didn't want anyone to interfere with his progress. "As long as no one bugs me while I'm practicing," he added.

No one did. Instead, people dotted the sidelines like

chalk marks waiting for Earl. There were autograph seekers who picked up any available scraps of paper. And there were countless sportswriters, photographers, and camera crews eager to record his every word. They had an endless stream of questions, and Earl answered them all.

"Next year," he said with a smile, "there'll be somebody else (in whom the press is interested). That's the way life is. And someday it'll be fourth down, and I won't be able to go. I'll want to, but I won't be able to. There'll be another kid born into this world who can."

Earl wasn't seeking publicity, but when corralled for an interview, he was patient.

"I'll play where Coach Phillips wants me to play," Earl responded to a reporter's query. "And I'll start when he thinks I'm ready to start, when I know the plays well enough. Meanwhile, I'm not gonna gripe about it."

Soon it was Bum's turn to be put on the spot by reporters. "Earl's just like everyone else," Bum insisted. "He'll play as he deserves to, as he earns it. I'd like to say we have a timetable all laid out, but we don't. It's going to take some time for him to adjust to pro ball, but if he's the best, we're certainly gonna want him in there."

Asked whether Campbell would line up at fullback or tailback, the Oiler coach responded, "After you get the ball in your hands, it doesn't make much difference where you're coming from. It's where you're going that counts."

During the first two weeks of training camp, Earl seemed to be going nowhere. On the practice field, he didn't show his shoulder and leg strength—the fearsome straight-arm or the great lightning zigzag moves that made him so difficult to tackle. Understandably, Oiler backfield coach Andy Bourgeois found this worrisome.

83

Earl autographs a football for a fan. (Ray Keeling)

Bum Phillips fields questions from reporters. (Tony Bullard)

The man in charge of all the running backs never doubted Earl's ability when the Oilers were trading for his draft rights. Now, Andy had a "funny impression of Earl." And it bothered him.

In a controlled scrimmage, Earl had his chance, but rather than spin out or dip and hit-and-go, Earl let men come into him and make a play. No longer was he the reckless runner everyone knew. Furthermore, in Earl's first competitive test—the rookie scrimmage against the Chiefs—he was unimpressive. Not only did he mishandle passes, but he came up with a scant 38 yards that took him 10 carries to achieve.

Certainly, players do tackle better in the pros, and Campbell had seldom been used as a pass receiver at Texas because the Wishbone isn't a passing formation. But he was staying after every practice and working on catching passes that were hurled out of a machine. Something was wrong. And Andy Bourgeois was sharp enough to guess what it was.

If Earl showed his explosiveness, his balance, and his strength, he would draw attention to himself. Equally important, he would appear far superior to the other rookies. Apparently, Earl didn't want to do that. When the coaches discussed the matter, they gambled on the fact that Earl was pacing himself, waiting for the veterans to arrive at camp. Once they were sharing the attention, Phillips and Bourgeoise felt sure that Earl would take off like an All-Pro who had been slow getting started.

When Earl was about to leave the dining hall on the first night the veterans were on the Angelo State campus, he heard someone bellow his name.

"Okay, Tyler Rose, let's hear it," demanded a veteran.

"C'mon, Earl!" urged Carl Mauck. "Entertain us. Sing your favorite song."

Embarrassed, Earl sang "The Eyes of Texas" in a monotone.

The next night, the veterans wanted more. This time Earl chose, "Mamas, Don't Let Your Babies Grow up to Be Cowboys." The veterans whooped and hollered! Although they were glad Earl was an Oiler, they didn't want him to know it yet.

The next night, Earl ate quickly and then headed for his fourth-floor room, where he locked himself in with his playbook until his 11:30 P.M. curfew.

He spent most of his evenings studying his playbook, aware that a lot of people were counting on him and that one wrong move on his part could mess up a whole play. There were hundreds of plays to learn; the Oilers moved the ball in as many complicated ways as they could manage. To be of maximum help to his team, Earl would have to be able to play two spots. In the I, he sometimes had to operate as the I back, and other times as the fullback. It wasn't easy for a rookie to learn so many new plays. Even a veteran player sometimes has problems with his routes.

During the next few weeks, Earl was often seen in the parking lot, walking through plays with his offensive lineman. Everyone was taking pains to coach him—even those who thought he might take over their jobs.

"I've got a lot to learn," Earl told reporters.

And he was learning more in practice every day. At night, he often closed his eyes and saw himself running plays. Before long, he looked like anything but a rookie.

"I sure am ready for game day to get here," Earl said. "I'm tired of camp. I want to get on the field and play."

17 / *The Football Championship of Texas*

There were fireworks in the Oilers' steamy locker room at Texas Stadium after the annual pre-season contest between Houston and Dallas—billed as "The Texas Super Bowl." Earl had done his best. What's more, he had shown the veterans that he belonged in the NFL. He had no trouble finding open spaces. Against Houston's most formidable opponent, the Super Bowl XII champion, Earl piled up 151 yards on a paltry 14 carries and scored on a 55-yard spring that was more than long enough to take the wind out of Dallas, 27–13.

"I didn't give Earl Campbell enough credit," said Cowboy safety Cliff Harris. "He's big and fast. I didn't know he could do it. But now I know. In fact, he's one of the best backs I've ever faced."

Clearly, Earl had shown that he deserved to move up. This was by far his finest pre-season performance. In the exhibition opener against the AFC champion Denver Broncos, Earl gained 29 yards in 12 attempts. He followed

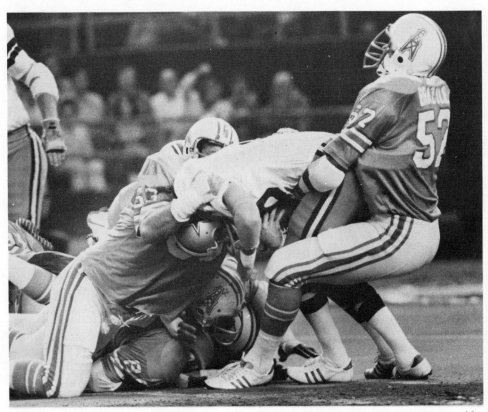

The Houston defense stops the Cowboys. (Sam Pierson, Jr.)

with only a slightly improved showing over Philadelphia. But he was learning more each week.

"He's running more under control than he was at first," said a beaming Bum Phillips. "He's doing better at picking his holes and then accelerating through them. This was the first time that he's had an opportunity to break one. He was real reckless tonight, with the first team line in there. Earl's a fine back. As good as you need to win."

Earl accepted the praise quietly. He refused to discuss his performance or to be forced into comparing his game with that of Dorsett, who had been held by the Oiler defense to 72 yards in 14 carries.

"I don't rate myself," declared Earl. "I'm out there to play football and let the people see and evaluate."

As soon as the Oilers were on a charter flight back to Houston, Carl Mauck began celebrating. He stood beside Earl Campbell's seat.

"All right, Tyler Rose!" Mauck shouted.

"Hey, man," Earl said softly, looking up with a grin. "I couldn't do it without you guys. You blocked real well. I was right on your tail on that touchdown. You know it?"

Mauck smiled and nodded. Never again would he force Earl to sing.

For the first time, Earl Campbell felt he was accepted by his teammates.

18 / *Houston Strikes It Rich*

When the 1978 football season opened, Earl was in the starting lineup, as a tailback in Houston's I-formation attack. Alongside him in the backfield was Tim Wilson, a second-year player from Maryland whose job was to block for Earl. Quarterback Dan Pastorini was calling the signals when the Oilers took on the Atlanta Falcons in Atlanta.

The first time Earl touched the football, he moved it two yards. The second time, he leapfrogged for six more yards. The third time, he grabbed a routine quick screen pass from Dan Pastorini and "took off like somebody stealing Mama's roses," according to Tommy Bonk of the *Houston Post*. Driving with his powerful stiff arm, Earl raced 73 yards for his first National Football League touchdown.

Earl outran four Falcon defenders to the goal line, his distance growing with every stride. Finally, Rick Byers dived after him from the ten, seconds before Earl had sailed into the end zone. Yet, when the final gun went off, the visitors from Texas were the disappointed 20–14 losers. Although Earl amassed 137 yards in his pro debut, it wasn't enough. Still, no one was blaming the Tyler Rose because

Earl is off and running. (Sam Pierson, Jr.)

his team didn't win. He had done what he could. In fact, he'd done more than his share.

Aside from drawing rave reviews from his own team-mates, Earl again impressed the competition. "I was hoping that if we got to him early, he'd cough the ball up like a lot of young players do," said Atlanta Coach Leeman Bennett. "But we hit him, hit him, hit him, and he never fumbled. He's going to be an exceptionally good NFL back."

Even with Earl on their team, it appeared that the Oilers would have an embarrassing second blotch on their record the next week in Missouri. Because they were trailing Kansas City 17–6 in the fourth period, they appeared to be almost certain losers.

"Keep plugging," Mauck told his teammates in the huddle, "or people are going to write us off."

Instead, people began taking note of their ground game. With time running out and Pastorini under pressure, he handed off to Campbell—not once or twice, but time and time again. Tucking the ball under his arm, racing against the clock, Earl began rolling up the big yardage—111, to be exact.

All week long, Earl had looked at films of Kansas City in action, hoping to learn all he could. Knowing how the Chiefs moved was helpful. "Looking at films, we felt they charged low," Earl said after his one- and two-yard thrusts into the end zone. "It was up to me to get over the top." And he did. Whereas few running backs would have had enough agility even to reach the scrimmage line in the same situation, Earl had the power necessary to score.

For Earl, sparking the offense was all in an afternoon's work. The record-setting collegian now led the NFL in rushing. Only two other rookies in the history of pro football had managed back-to-back 100-yard games in their first starts: the New York Giants' Zollie Toth in 1950 and Hall-of-Famer Alan Ameche. But no one had accomplished the feat in more than twenty years.

Now, the football-loving people of Texas poured into the Astrodome, talking excitedly about their home-grown phenomenon. They soon saw what they had come for—their daring rookie lead the Oilers to a nerve-wracking 20–19 win over the San Francisco Forty-niners. As the jubilant fans drove away in their cars, O. J. ("The Juice") Simpson made a prediction: "I saw Earl play last year," he said, "and I told people then that he was the best running back in college football. Now, I'm predicting he'll

The Derrick Dolls, Houston's cheerleaders. (Tony Bullard)

Heisman Trophy winner John Cappelleti (22) carries the ball for the Los Angeles Rams. (Sam Pierson, Jr.)

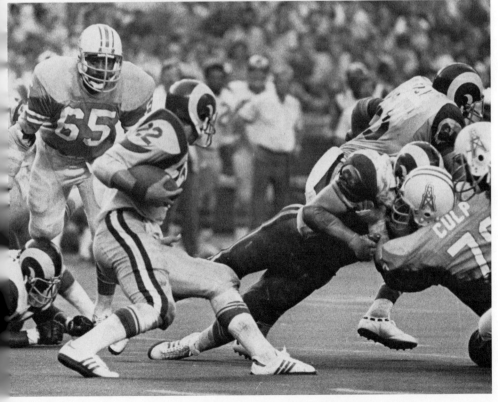

go farther faster than anybody in the history of pro football." (As a rookie, Simpson had gained 698 yards.)

But not in the next few weeks. Although Earl wore pantyhose for extra protection against muscle pulls, he suffered a pulled hamstring when Houston collided with Los Angeles.

And he wasn't happy about sitting out Houston's 16–13 win over Cleveland or about the fact that his prospects looked grim for the Oilers' match-up with Oakland.

As it happened, a scant sixty minutes before game time, Earl got clearance to go against the Raiders. The decision to play him was made after Andy Bourgeois watched Earl in a pre–pre-game workout. When the offensive backfield coach saw that Earl was able to loosen up and run hard for the first time in two weeks, he talked with Bum Phillips. Together, they decided to play their prize rookie, but they didn't put him in the starting lineup. Ronnie Coleman started in his place; then Earl quickly took over.

"I didn't feel confident on the first two or three carries," Campbell revealed after finishing the day with 103 yards on 26 totes. "After that, everything was all right."

Well, not quite. With less than six minutes remaining in the third quarter, the upset-bent Oilers were leading the Oakland Raiders 17–7. The Texas team was in possession of the ball and just four yards from a touchdown—one that might have put a mark in the Oiler win column except for what happened next. Pastorini handed off to Earl. Then 52,500 disbelieving Californians saw Raider end Dave Browning reach out and strip the ball from Houston's super rookie just as Earl began his cut into the end zone. Instantaneously, strong safety Charley Phillips scooped up the ball and returned it 96 yards, untouched by anyone wearing Columbia blue. Houston was in trouble—big trouble, and things got worse, not better.

With 42 seconds left in the game, the Raiders finished it off as Dave Casper grabbed a winning touchdown pass, fired from quarterback Kenny Stabler's swift left arm.

"I'm going to have some bad games down the line," said Earl, after the 17–21 loss. "I just have to make sure that I have more good ones. Still, a fumble is hard to forget."

Seven games into his rookie season, Earl had already reassured his coaches and teammates that the Oilers hadn't misjudged him.

"Earl is everything we thought he would be," said Bum Phillips, after his team's 17–10 win over Buffalo, in which Earl went 105 yards on 19 carries. "He has the ability to separate himself from Earl Campbell, the hero. He's not a hero to himself."

"Earl's very conscientious," Andy Bourgeois told reporters. "It gets to him real bad when he makes a mistake. He's got such a low profile, unlike most Heisman Trophy winners, who wear flashy clothes, buy big cars, and lead pretty fast lifestyles. Earl's profile is about as slow as he walks. He's got two gears—crawling and exploding."

Without a doubt, Earl shifted into high gear for Houston's next three games. In one, some of his teammates sputtered. As a result, Earl labored in vain against Cincinnati, as Houston fell 13–28. But the team did beat the mighty Pittsburgh Steelers 24–17, and the Cleveland Browns 14–10. Against the Steelers and Browns, the Oilers made comebacks their trademark.

In what was the Oilers' most remarkable comeback to

date, the team spotted the New England Patriots 23 points in the first half and then miraculously regrouped during intermission to come from zero and win a 26–23 thriller.

"When we fell behind like this in the past," said defensive end Elvin Bethea, "we used to fold and then keep on going on down the hill. Then we'd go into the next game and go straight down the hill farther. But now we have confidence in our offense, and the offense has confidence in itself. Earl is an inspiration. When we get the ball to him, we feel he can do it."

One thing was certain. These weren't the same Oilers, regardless of the situation they were in. No one was quitting, folding, or giving up. Instead, Houston was running proud and extremely confident. Earl was giving his team both a solid running game and self-respect. Justifiably, *Sports Illustrated* slated Houston's spectacular rookie for its cover and then suggested that the Oilers change their name to "the Houston Earlers." The reason for this was obvious when the team went against the Miami Dolphins on "Monday Night Football."

In one of the most splendid nights in Oiler history, a nationwide television audience of millions saw Earl paving the way to an exciting 35–30 victory by rushing 199 yards on 28 carries. His final tote was an 81-yard peel to his fourth touchdown of the night—the touchdown that won the game for the Oilers. While Earl gasped for breath in the end zone, the Astrodome rocked with applause in a sea of blue-and-white pompons, waved by cheering Texans. Earl was the player that victory-starved Houstonians had been waiting for, and they let him know it. In fact, they were so busy shouting that they failed to notice that it was several minutes before Earl was able to make it back to the Oiler bench.

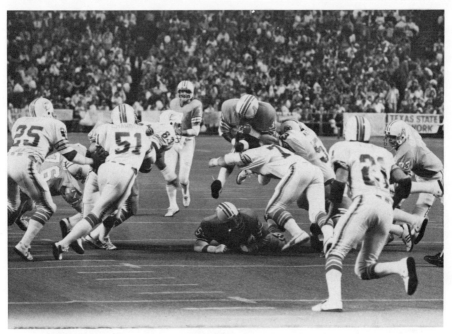

Earl jumps his center, Carl Mauck (55), to pick up three extra yards against Miami. (Wide World Photos)

Earl congratulates Tim Wilson (45) and Ronnie Coleman (47). (Tony Bullard)

When Earl was tired, he usually hid the fact. Against Miami, however, Tim Wilson noted, "Earl looked dead a few times. Then he'd take off and run again."

For Earl's running, Wilson deserved some credit. Tim Wilson was like an icebreaker opening a ship's channel, clearing Earl's way down the field. The Oiler fullback specialized in reading defenses quickly. He had done a lot of this for his tailback at Maryland, where he was primarily a blocking back and short-yardage getter.

"I just follow Tim," Earl often said. "Wherever he goes, I go. I know that's where the hole's gonna be."

The coaches also appreciated the way Wilson scanned the defense. "Tim makes a split-second decision on who to block better than anybody I've ever coached," Andy Bourgeois said. "He's able to look around on every play and see who needs help. If everybody's where they're supposed to be, he goes where he's supposed to. If not, he improvises. And he always guesses right."

"What about the dinner?" defensive coordinator Ed Biles asked Earl above the roar in the Oiler dressing room after the win.

"You remembered!" drawled Earl.

Biles gave Earl the statistics for inspection. Dolphin Delvin Williams had gained a slim 73 yards against Houston's defense, giving him 1,130 yards for the year. And Earl's 199-yard effort upped him to 1,143 big ones—enough acreage to snatch the league's rushing title from Williams. With three games to go, Earl was only 19 yards shy of being the leading rookie rusher of all time. (San Diego's Don Woods had set the record with 1,164 yards in 1974).

Shortly before the Oilers took the field, Robert Brazile

called across the locker room to Earl: "We'll get four touchdowns from you tonight!"

"And you guys will keep Williams under 100 yards," Campbell retorted. "If you do, I'll take you to dinner."

Delirously happy Houstonians were walking to the parking lot, as Earl smiled and said, "Tell me the night, the time, whatever. The dinner's on me. Y'all deserve it!"

Earl also took his offensive line, plus Tim Wilson, to a Japanese steak house for dinner. It was his way of expressing appreciation for the blocks that enabled him to become the first Oiler to gain 1,000 yards since Hoyle Granger in 1967.

During the evening, Earl's teammates talked about picking up the check because they couldn't have been more elated that he was on their team. As far as they were concerned, Earl could do no wrong.

As it turned out, there was no arguing over the bill. When Earl requested it, he was told that an Oiler fan at a nearby table had already paid the tab. It was the man's way of thanking the Oilers for giving Houston something to cheer about. The Oiler win over Miami had tightened the race for the five American Conference playoff spots. And it appeared more certain than ever that Coach Phillips would finally get to wear his cowboy hat and best boots (blue-and-white checked ones) to the games.

Then Houston did it the hard way again and stormed from behind to a 17–10 triumph over the Cincinnati Bengals.

A pelting rain—known as a Texas "frog strangler"—kept 8,086 fans from their seats in Houston's covered Astrodome. Still, Earl kept dishing it out, thundering ahead with another 100-yard showing, making it clear that the

Earl holds out a stiff arm to protect himself from Bengals' Scott Perry (32), while being pursued by Jim LeClair (55) and Wilson Whitley (75). (UPI)

"souped-up" Oilers were a team to be reckoned with after the Bengals had bolted to a quick 10–0 lead in the first half.

Before Earl joined the Oilers, Houston's offense was composed mainly of ho-hum drives up the middle for little or no gain. The drives were predictably followed by a Pastorini pass to one of his favorite receivers—either Ken Burrough or Billy "White Shoes" Johnson. There had been little mystery about what the Oilers would do.

Now, Houston had an improved line and balanced attack, which enabled the team to come from behind in eight of their nine victories. Earl's brute force and breakaway speed, together with his gliding balance, forced the opposition to key on him. This opened up the Oilers' passing game. Pastorini was netting the best statistics of his eight-year career. To date, he had connected on 55.3 percent of his 295 passes for a high of 2,080 yards and 12 touchdowns. Furthermore, even when the defense was keying hard on Earl, it often did no good. If short yardage was needed, the Oilers went to Earl, and he usually scooted enough yards to get it.

So far, he had been given the ball 24 times in third-down situations with three yards or less to go for a first down. Eighteen times he picked up the crucial yardage. And on one third-and-seven play, Earl galloped for a 73-yard touchdown run. Equally amazing, on fourth down, he was handed the ball four times and gained an average of 12.2 yards each time.

"It's a blessing he's on our side," said Elvin Bethea. "It's a blessing not to have to tackle him." Then in a serious vein, he added, "What's happened here is that Earl fits in like the last piece of the puzzle. We've needed him for years."

None would disagree. After four straight victories, the Oilers now had a 9–4 record.

"I thought Earl would be the kind of runner he is," Coach Phillips told the press after his team whipped Cincinnati. "But he's really surprised us with his blocking, faking, and pass protecting. He's a good run blocker when the other guy's got the football. He's got absolutely no regard for his body or anybody else's body."

Earl was simply doing his job. However, doing his job meant that his competitors had to work overtime because he was a menace on the field and ran them ragged.

Almost everyone in Houston thinks "Campbell is Souper" and is a member of the "Houston Earlers" fan club. (Sam Pierson, Jr.)

"He's like three players in one," claimed Gary Burley, the Bengals' defensive end, who spent all afternoon trying to stop Earl from gaining 122 yards on 27 carries and from becoming the leading rookie rusher in NFL history. "He's got the strength of Jim Brown, the acceleration of O. J. Simpson, and the second effort of Minnesota's David Osborne."

"Facing Earl twice a year is too much," insisted Bengal defensive tackle Eddie Edwards. "He was running loose all over the field, and we couldn't control him."

"But how can he keep that up?" wondered Burley. "I hope he doesn't intend to run that hard his whole career. If he does, I don't see how he can last as long as he should. Maybe I'm wrong," Burley said. "Maybe he's Superman."

Other players were also wondering out loud how much longer Houston's powerful running back could avoid injury if the Oilers continued to rely on him so greatly. Two years? Three years?

But Oiler receiver Ken Burrough said, "The way I look at it, he's putting some longevity in my career. I figured I didn't have but maybe three years left. But with him around carrying the ball, I'll be around a lot longer than I thought. When you've got a guy like that, you're crazy to throw the ball as much as we have in the past. Earl's my man."

Nevertheless, when Earl watched game films, he noticed the way a player delivered a blow, the way he was tackled and landed on his head. Then he often realized that he could have been hurt during a particular play. But during a game, he never worried about getting hurt. "I concentrate on getting to the hole I'm supposed to," said Earl. "I don't want to make any mistakes out there."

Concentrating was exactly what he was doing—concentrating on beating the 11–2 Pittsburgh Steelers for the second time in one year. Since the National Football League-American Football League merger in 1970, no team in the division had beaten Pittsburgh twice in the same season. Now, the Steelers were two games ahead of the Oilers in the Central Division. What's more, almost everybody who lived outside Houston was betting that Pittsburgh would represent the American Football Conference in Super Bowl XIII.

"Don't talk to me about that," exclaimed Oiler quarterback Dan Pastorini. "The playoffs, the Super Bowl. That stuff doesn't matter now. Nobody on this team is looking past Pittsburgh."

"When we play them," Bum Phillips declared, "it's not a game—it's a collision. The team with the most Band-Aids wins."

Even with crates of Band-Aids in both teams' locker rooms, Donnie Shell said, "I don't know if anybody's ready for Earl Campbell." Shell had been knocked unconscious in a collision with Earl the first time the two teams met.

As it happened, it was Earl who wasn't ready for quick, hard-hitting Donnie Shell. The rookie halfback never saw Shell's helmet driving at his rib cage as Earl was twisting out of Mike Wagner's grip. With 1:03 left in the first quarter, Shell rammed into Earl—putting the NFL's leading rusher out of the game and the Oilers out of running order.

When Earl fell to the ground, the crowd grew still. In the hush, fans focused their binoculars on the Astrodome floor. Clearly, Earl was having difficulty breathing. In addi-

Earl is helped from the field by Tim Wilson (45) and Mike Barber (86). (Wide World Photos)

tion, he couldn't lift his right arm to be helped off the field.

When the Oilers returned for the second half, Earl wasn't with them. Later, when fans spotted him walking slowly out of the tunnel, they gave him a standing ovation.

Although Earl had a broken rib, he hoped that he could "gut" it out. But when he asked teammate Teddy Thompson to bang on his shoulder pads, Earl nearly collapsed.

Indeed, the Astrodome was no place for the fainthearted. Before the afternoon ended, eleven Houston players needed attention from the Oiler medical staff. Pittsburgh, too, knew they'd been at war. The Houston trainer likened the battle between the Oilers and the Steelers to World War III.

Most severely injured was rookie receiver, Mike Renfo, who finished his first pro season with 26 receptions for 339 yards, two touchdowns, and knee surgery scheduled for the following morning. Cornerback Willie Alexander lost a tooth and broke his jaw. Others who were flattened included noseguard Curley Culp, with a pinched nerve; linebacker Robert Brazile, with a muscle tear; and linebacker Steve Kinger, with a sliced foot. Tight end Mike Barber dislocated a shoulder, and Dan Pastorini broke three ribs.

"That was the toughest street fight I was ever in," Pastorini said, after the Steelers wiped up the green Astroturf with Houston and wrapped up the division crown for the seventh year in a row.

In all his 31 years of coaching, Bum Phillips had never seen such a "hammer-and-tong" game. "We didn't have enough Band-Aids," sighed Bum (a name bestowed upon him by his sister who could not pronounce "brother" when she was two). "It was the best game I've ever seen played defensively, the most physical game I've ever seen."

Said Chuck Noll, the Steeler coach, "It was a big game. Houston wanted it; we wanted it. It was a test of wills."

After directing the Steelers to a 13–3 win, Terry Bradshaw said, "I've played tough games that were full of fights, arguments, and cheap shots, like against Dallas or Cleveland. But I've never played in a game as tough as this against a team I respected."

Worthy of esteem or not, the Oilers fizzled without Earl. Before he was hurt, Earl was running well—up, around, and over anyone who stood in his way. But he didn't stand a chance against the Steelers.

"Our defense was waiting for him," volunteered Bradshaw.

"We were geared to stop him," confessed "Mean" Joe Green, the Steeler tackle whose nickname is self-explanatory. "If there is such a thing as a superstar, Earl's it."

There were now two teams in the AFC conference with better records than the Oilers'—Pittsburgh at 12–2 and the New England Patriots at 10–4. Denver and Miami dittoed Houston's 9–5 showing, while Oakland, Seattle, and the New York Jets were 8–6.

The possibility of Houston making the playoffs in 1978 looked dim. The Oilers were in critical condition, and, unfortunately, everyone—including their next opponents, the New Orleans Saints—knew it. This was owing to the fact that each pro football team must file an injury report every Wednesday and Friday with the NFL office. After all 28 reports are compiled, they are wired to each club and released to both major wire services: the Associated Press and United Press International.

To compound problems, the Houston team at its healthiest, couldn't handle the Saints in their own back yard, the Astrodome. In the final pre-season game in Houston, New Orleans had whipped the Oilers easily, 17–3. Then, the Saints had been just revving up. Now, they were 6–8, a twelve-year organization high.

Nonetheless, the Oilers were determined to fight their way into the playoffs. And that's exactly what Houston

Earl in backfield with Pastor (7) and Wilson (45). (Tc Bullard)

Terry Bradshaw. (Pittsb Steelers)

did—sporting their black-and-blue marks, as well as their team's traditional Columbia blue, white, and red.

By combining their 17–12 win over New Orleans with losses by Oakland, Seattle, and the New York Jets, Houston locked up its very first playoff berth in nine hard years after being down a nervous 10–zip.

All that is history, but at the time, Earl had not been his usual dashing self. "I was never full speed," he admitted, remembering that when the Oilers needed his help most in the final quarter, he had failed to gain.

Fortunately for the team, Pastorini hit newcomer Robert Woods on a second down for an 80-yard scoring expedition that turned out to be the winning touchdown.

"Once I saw Woods in the clear, I knew nobody would catch him," said Pastorini, whose broken rib cage, like Campbell's, was carefully guarded by a special inflated and padded vest under his jersey.

Actually, until the week before the game, Woods had been working at a children's center in Little Rock, Arkansas. Coach Andy Bourgeois had scouted him at Grambling in the spring. But Kansas City took him in the fifth round before Houston could draft him as planned. When Woods was cut, the Oilers thought they had plenty of receivers. As it turned out, the front office was wrong.

Then the injury-plagued team began tracking Woods down, hoping to enlist his help. Finally, the 5-feet 6-inch 160-pounder was handed a uniform after he successfully caught all his practice punts during the Pittsburgh pre-game warm-up.

"He's so small," Bum said, "when he showed up at the dressing room for the Pittsburgh game, the guard wouldn't let him in the door. I don't know, but I suspect that's why he didn't make the Kansas City team last summer."

Prior to the New Orleans game, some of his teammates didn't even know he was on their team. Special teams coach John Paul Young divulged, "They'd ask me, 'Who is that little guy?' I didn't know much about him, either, except that he seemed to have good hands, strong nerves, and we timed him in a 4.5 40 Friday."

By Monday morning, few Houstonians would need to ask, "Who is Robert Woods?" He was a media event, the talk of the town.

The Oilers needed a victory in the season's finale to clinch the home-field advantage in the American Football Conference, wild-card playoff game against Miami on December 24. Therefore, there was concern all week about where the team would be spending Christmas Eve. But instead of worrying about this, the Oilers should have been thankful they didn't have to fly to San Diego. And they were grateful—after the Chargers drilled the Oilers 45–24 and wrecked Houston's plans for staying at home.

The 45 embarrassing points the Chargers scored were the most notched on Houston since Minnesota's 51–10 win in 1974. Even in 1972 and 1973—grim 1–13 seasons—the Oiler team records showed they allowed 45 points only once per year.

"I want to go to Miami," said place kicker Toni Fritsch. "But, not now. It's too early."

A win would have meant that the Oilers wouldn't see sunny Miami until they advanced through the playoff steps and into Super Bowl XIII—the biggest game of the year. It was scheduled to be played in Miami on January 21, 1979, to decide the football championship of the world.

After the way Houston looked against the Chargers, it was doubtful that the Oilers would be going anywhere. However, Dan Pastorini disagreed: "We just went from the penthouse to the outhouse—quick," he declared, while packing his knee in ice.

Adding to Dan's problems, Earl had failed to pick up his audible call. This had forced Dan to keep the ball himself and had resulted in his being injured.

The star running back still had his weaknesses. His pass receiving was only fair. There were also many times during the year when Earl failed to get into the blocking scheme. "He'd make the wrong read on a block and cut the direction he shouldn't have cut," Coach Bourgeois said. "He'd make four yards on brute strength, so not many people would notice. Give him a few more seasons and he won't make that mistake. It bothers Earl when he doesn't get the yards he should. He figures the linemen work hard to give him the opportunity, and that he's letting them down when he doesn't take advantage of it. One of the beauties of working with Earl is that you know he'll work harder at doing it right the next time. He has a great capacity for getting better. Some backs will complain about carrying the ball too much or not carrying it enough. You never hear that from him. He's too busy thinking about how he can improve."

After the showing against San Diego, it was clear that all of the Oilers had room for improvement.

"Let's face it. We stunk up the Astrodome," Willie Alexander said bluntly. "By the end of the third quarter, I expected to see the fans with clothespins on their noses. When football players lose, what they hate maybe more than anything is waking up Monday morning and having to read the sports pages or listen to the sports reports. They get up, go to the mirror with one eye open, then slowly open the other eye. When they look in the mirror, they don't like what they see, either."

"I don't know if we thought they'd roll over and play dead, or if we were looking ahead to Miami," said free safety Mike Reinfeldt, whose secondary twice intercepted Dan Fouts's passes (but failed to stop 19 of Fouts's 38 others) and let him fire four touchdown passes.

"It was our best game against a strong, physical, well-coached football team," said Don Coryell, who took over as coach of the Chargers when Tommy Prothro was ejected and San Diego seemingly hopelessly down 1–4. "In spite of the score, Houston's mighty tough. You saw that down on the goal line."

The Oilers had stalled a Charger drive at the Houston one. But other than that, the day was San Diego's—a day the Oilers wanted to forget.

"These bad games hurt bad, real bad," Coach Phillips said. "But I've had a whole lot of good ones this year, too. You've gotta take the bitter with the sweet. It goes with the job."

This Earl learned, as the 1977 NCAA rushing champion became the 1978 NFL titlist, rushing for an awesome 1,450 yards. Earl was the first rookie to lead the NFL in rushing since Jimmy Brown in 1957. Earl broke or tied eight individual Oiler records, and his seven 100-yard games tied Hoyle Granger's career mark.

In 1978, Chicago's Walter Payton finished the season with 1,395 yards, while Philadelphia's Wilbert Montgomery gained 1,334 and Miami's Delvin Williams earned 1,252.

19 / *How Earl Became the Leader*

Game	Carries	Yardage	Average	Longest Gain	Touchdowns
Atlanta	15	137	9.1	73	1
Kansas City	22	107	5.0	22	2
San Francisco	25	78	3.1	16	1
Los Angeles	13	77	5.9	16	0
Cleveland			DID NOT PLAY		
Oakland	25	104	4.1	23	0
Buffalo	19	105	5.5	45	0
Pittsburgh	21	89	4.2	23	3
Cincinnati	18	102	5.6	47	0
Cleveland	19	71	3.7	15	0
New England	24	74	3.1	9	1
Miami	28	199	7.1	81	4
Cincinnati	27	122	4.5	17	0
Pittsburgh	7	41	5.8	11	0
New Orleans	25	67	2.7	8	1
San Diego	14	77	5.5	50	0
Totals	302	1,450	4.8	81	13

Clearly, the Oilers would have welcomed a week off after four exhibition and sixteen regular season games, but under the playoff specifications, that sort of luxury wasn't afforded wild-card teams. Fittingly, the deck was stacked against any team that made it into the playoffs as runner-up in its division. In any case, it appeared to all concerned that Houston had already taken a vacation in the Astro-dome while playing San Diego. With that humiliating event in the immediate past, it was no wonder that the Oilers attended strictly to business when they arrived in Miami. This time it was "do or die" in the first round of the NFL playoffs.

Miami had a reputation for stopping the big man. However, mention of this caused Bum Phillips to remind people that Miami knew about Earl in the first game but didn't stop him.

Nor did they stop him in this game. Earl traveled 86 yards in 26 carries. More important, the Dolphin defense was keying on him. And when a defense keyed on Earl, it opened up the play-action passes. As a result, Dan Pastorini had the finest hour of his eight-year career in Miami. He hurled 20 of 30 passes that were right on target for a glossy 306 yards during a game in which Houston was a six-point underdog.

The Oilers did win, 17–9. And the merriest of Christmases was celebrated one day early in Houston town.

Bum Phillips acknowledged the cheers of Houston fans in Miami by tossing his straw Texan hat into the crowd. Then, when the team arrived home, fans ripped Earl's shirt right off his back. And more than 3,000 people mobbed the Oilers after their bus rolled into the parking lot. In short, Houston was overcome by "Oilermania."

When Earl was safely in his van, a compact car blocked his way until the crowd picked up the car and removed it. Needless to say, Earl was grateful, for the Oilers were in a hurry. They had only a week to prepare for round two of the playoffs—a meeting with the New England Patriots in Foxboro, Massachusetts.

Dan Pastorini at work. (Sam Pierson, Jr.)

For the Patriot game, Oiler equipment manager Greg Doramus packed two different types of gloves: deerskin for players who would handle the ball, and wool for the linemen. He also shopped for long-sleeved undershirts, thermal underwear, caps, capes, three different kinds of cleated shoes, heating packs, salve (to protect the players' skin against the biting cold), hand warmers, and pantyhose for Earl.

Then Houston was on its way. Pastorini completed a record 12 of 15 passes for 200 yards. Once the Tyler Rose changed his cleats to the kind the Patriots were wearing, he blasted ahead 27 times for 118 yards, including Houston's fourth touchdown. And the Oilers upset New England 31–14.

Then fate interceded, and the weather played a cruel trick. After clergymen cut short their Sunday sermons so that their congregations could be in front of their television sets to view the American Football Conference Championship game in Pittsburgh, Three Rivers Stadium was blanketed in sleet and snow. And the Steelers set up a Super Bowl meeting with Dallas by chilling Houston 34–5. For the Oilers, the season was over.

But no one would have known it by the sound of the 50,000 cheering Houstonians who welcomed the Oilers home at the "World's Largest Pep Rally" in the Astrodome. "Nowhere, but nowhere were there fans like those in Houston, Texas. And never before was there a rookie like Earl," the wire services reported.

Earl Campbell had united his adopted city.

"I've learned a lot about pro football," Campbell told his fans. "I found out that the people who play this game are human beings. I used to stereotype the pro player. I'd

116

see a guy on TV and say, 'I bet you can't get close to him.' But that's not the way it is in the pros. The players are ordinary people, just like me. They want the same things everybody wants, like going to the Super Bowl, just like high school athletes want to go to State. They want people to respect them for what they are, not as football players.

"It was a good year," he continued. "I wanted the Super Bowl, but you can't always have what you want. My goal is to win the Super Bowl before I'm through, and when I'm through, I hope I'm still a Houston Oiler!"

Fifty thousand roaring fans stun the Oilers with a warm reception when they return from the American Football Conference Championship game in Pittsburgh. (Sam Pierson, Jr.)

EARL CAMPBELL'S 27 POST-SEASON AWARDS

AP Player of the Year * AP All-Pro * UPI All-AFC * *Sporting News* All-AFC * *Pro Football Weekly* All-NFL * *Pro Football Weekly* All-AFC * *Pro Football Weekly* Top Offensive Player in NFL * *Pro Football Weekly* Offensive Rookie of the Year * NEA Awarded Jim Thorpe Trophy (MVP in NFL) * NEA Awarded Bert Bell Trophy (MVP of the Year in NFL) * NEA Awarded Third Down Trophy (MVP of Oilers, voted by teammates) * NEA All-Pro * Selected to play in Pro Bowl * *Football News* AFC Player of the Year * Pro Football Writers Player of the Year * Pro Football Writers All-Pro * Mutual Broadcasting Company NFL Player of the Year * *Football Digest* NFL Player of the Year * *Football Digest* Top Running Back in NFL * *Football Digest* Offensive Rookie of the Year * Freshen Up Gum Pro Football Hall of Fame Rookie of the Year in AFC (voted by fans) * Bill Ennis Award (given by Houston area sportswriters and sportscasters) * Seagram's Seven Crown of Sports Outstanding Player in NFL * Field Scovell Award of Dallas Sports Association * Texaco Youth Award for Pro Football * *Sporting News* AFC Player of the Year * *Sporting News* AFC Rookie of the Year *

Index

120

121